Colin Mudie
Sailing Ships

Colin Mudie
Sailing Ships

**DESIGNS & RE-CREATIONS OF GREAT SAILING SHIPS ~
FROM ANCIENT GREECE TO THE PRESENT DAY**

ADLARD COLES NAUTICAL
London

CONTENTS

Thanks vi

Introduction 1

Floating Hypotheses 5
An approach to re-creations of ancient vessels

Sailing Ships and Yachts 8
Sailing performance in the past, and now

Galleys 10
The 'motor-sailers' of antiquity

Materials 12
The basis of construction

Lines Plans 15
The development of shape

ARGO 18
Jason's galley re-created for Tim Severin
~ 13th Century BC & 1984

HSU FU 30
Sailing the Pacific in a bamboo raft
3rd Century BC & 1993

LIBURNIAN 37
1st Century AD Roman warship

BRENDAN 42
A leather-skinned curragh for an Atlantic crossing
~ 6th Century AD & 1976/77

SUTTON HOO 51
The 7th Century AD ship from a Suffolk barrow

SOHAR 55
Sindbad's dhow ~ 9th Century AD & 1980/81

MATTHEW 63
John Cabot's ship for his Newfoundland voyage
~ 1497 & 1997

AILEACH 78
Design for a West Highland birlinn
~ 16th Century & 1991/92

MARY ROSE 86
A new look at Henry VIII's flagship ~ 16th Century

H.M.S. VICTORY 90
Nelson's great ship ~ 18th Century

DUNBRODY 92
An Irish barque of the 19th Century ~ 1845 & 2000

CUTTY SARK 103
The clipper ship at Greenwich ~ 19th Century

T.S. ROYALIST 106
The Sea Cadets' brig ~ 1971

T.S. VARUNA 118
Royalist's sister ship ~ 1979

S.T.S. LORD NELSON 120
The barque everyone can sail in ~ 1985

S.T.S. YOUNG ENDEAVOUR 139
Britain's Bicentennial gift to Australia ~ 1987

K.L.D. TUNAS SAMUDERA 151
Young Endeavour's Malaysian sister ship ~ 1989

I.N.S. TARANGINI 154
Lord Nelson's Indian Navy sister ship ~ 1997

THE CADLAND SHIP 161
A great sailing ship for the nation

Epilogue 164

Glossary 166

Further Reading 169

Index 170

Published 2000 by Adlard Coles Nautical
an imprint of A & C Black (Publishers) Ltd
35 Bedford Row, London WC1R 4JH
www.adlardcoles.co.uk

Copyright © Colin Mudie 2000

The right of Colin Mudie to be identified as the author of this work
has been asserted by him in accordance with the Copyright, Design
and Patents Act 1998.

Illustrations © Colin Mudie 2000 unless otherwise credited

ISBN 0-7136-5324-8

A CIP catalogue record for this book is available from the British Library.

Typeset in 11 on 14pt Galliard.

Printed and bound in Italy
by G. Canale & C. S.p.A.

THANKS

One great pleasure in making up this book has been the opportunity to review how much I have enjoyed working with so many people on so many projects. It would perhaps take a whole volume to name them all and I would just like them to be aware of my thanks. I do, however, note my gratitude to some of those (in alphabetical order) who lead the list: Wallace Clark, Soli Contractor, Maldwin Drummond, Chris Rudd, Morin Scott, Tim Severin and Sarah Waters.

I am very conscious that it is the photographs and visuals that are the prime attraction and would specifically like to thank: Nathan Benn, Joe Beynon, the late Miles Clark, John Egan, Richard Greenhill, Lou Lyddon, Ian Mainsbridge, Rosemary, and especially Max. I also thank the Victoria & Albert Museum for permission to use the picture of the Trajan column frieze, the Editor of *Yachting World* for permission to use the Max Millar drawing of the *Cutty Sark*, the Wolfson Unit MTIA at Southampton University for permission to use the picture of *Lord Nelson* in the wind tunnel and the family of Charles Munro for permission to use his paintings of the *Jubilee Barque* and *Young Endeavour*.

Arthur Saluz must have a special paragraph of thanks for the contribution his visuals have made to our professional lives over many years as well as for the magnificent specimens of his work which enhance this book.

Those who know how our office functions will also understand that my total thanks must go to our 'in house' team without whom there would not have been any such fascinating projects, including this one.

Colin Mudie
Lymington

INTRODUCTION

The wheel is often put forward as man's greatest invention. Mariners think that it really only came into its own when it was shipped onboard sailing vessels as a steering aid. I was going to put forward the proposition that the sailing ship is one of the greatest products of the human race. A moment's thought, however, and the realisation is that this is far too modest. The sailing ship does not even have to contest the top slot. What other combination of natural materials, natural forces and human skills has developed into anything like it since the world began? A sailing ship has to work at the interface of the two most complex and sometimes violent fluid environments in the world and at the same time to provide a vehicle for two-dimensional space exploration, war and commerce. You can see that a simple wheel rolling along a muddy bit of land is a zero contestant.

Of course, there is technical accretion and modern skills with the electron and space travel and so on. Perhaps someday something in these areas will be recognised as a really major achievement but, taking the materials and technologies available, the sailing ship will require a great deal of catching up.

Our fascination with the ships of antiquity springs from another facet of which we find little cognisance or appreciation these days. That is that they were often of such a high technical standard that they were sometimes streets ahead of our modern approach to design. We were so surprised at what we began to see in the earliest of ships that we enquired about the development of human brainpower. The answer from a top anthropologist was that there has not been any noticeable increase since the agrarian revolution some seven thousand years ago. So there we are, one mystery explained. The ship, the top artefact of top communities, would have been the subject for the top brains in design, construction and use, and those brains would be the equivalent of those we now employ for modern space travel.

The other mystery was why one could detect a positive decline in the breadth of the modern technical approach. We thought that this was likely to be due to the onset of naval architecture, engineering calculations and computers. Up until naval architecture became a serious discipline the ship was designed directly by the builder who controlled every aspect and was directly responsible for its performance to the owners. Naval architecture in practice involves a third party who communicates specific requirements of build and form to the builder. With the best will and application in the world this cannot cover every aspect and inevitably there is likely to be a communication gap. One might then look at engineering calculations involved in the design of ships since Victorian times.

The stern badge carved by Norman Gaches, on the transom of *T. S. Royalist*. His work can also be seen on *Lord Nelson, Young Endeavour* and *Tunas Samudera*, and many other ships. Photo: Max

These again restrict the general appreciation of the work to those items which can be accessed through a calculation procedure. The computer, brilliant as it is in calculation, only calculates those items with which it has been programmed. Each step in the technology graph, greeted at the time as a great technical advance, contains some initial restrictions to be followed in due course by the development of wider and better assessments. At each step, however, it seems likely that some design factors may just have slipped through the cracks. It probably does not matter and the evidence to that is all around us in that modern ships are entirely competent, and safer perhaps than at any other time. There are these other aspects and it is, we think, valuable to have our eyes opened to them. Add to the overall situation the malformations of modern ships to optimise them to the taxing authorities and the not always beneficial hull design requirements of blanket safety regulations. Also take onboard that a century of yacht racing rules has stamped a historically unusual view of optimum sailing efficiencies and form on the boating world and you will see how fascinating we find it to be able to look well astern at the technical beauties of the ancients.

I should at this stage mention a neighbour when we lived in London and pay him a somewhat belated tribute for his part in opening our eyes to these possibilities of the past. Commander Geoffrey Bowles had been a gunnery officer in the Victorian navy and served under sail. As a gunner brought up on muzzleloaders he was a bit deaf and visits to him were by invitation. He was a considerable advocate of square rig in the days long before it again became

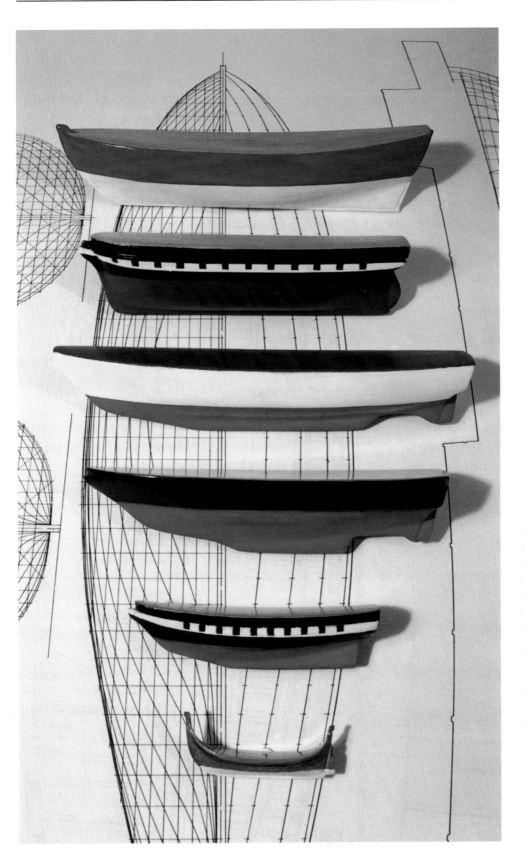

'Pocket' models, to scale, which I have made of some of the ships in the book. They help everyone, including me, to appreciate the differences in length and shape. And they are useful to have in my pocket when people ask 'what are you doing now?' From the top: *Mary Rose, Dunbrody, Tarangini, Young Endeavour, Royalist, Aileach.*
PHOTO: MAX

fashionable. To make the case he would re-rig his flat to illustrate the points that he would make to us. His broom and bedspread served as a squaresail with which he would demonstrate the ease of, for instance, 'clewing up'; other furniture stood in for Bentinck booms, Jarvis brace winches and fiferails. On one occasion he showed how easy it was to roller furl a squaresail and how it could easily be done single handed by 'the girl Mary'. We understood he was replanning square rig so that the girl Mary without further assistance could handle it. It is notable that some forty years later the girl Mary equivalent is to be found, doing her stuff, onboard every square rigger in the tall ships' events.

I would also mention George Naish of the Greenwich Maritime Museum who, looking back, was a major prompt into our investigating the wider aspects of sailing ship design from our rather narrow vision of modern yacht design. It was typical of him that when he wrote his will he left me, no doubt with his tongue in cheek, a pair of very comprehensive and old books on sailing ship design.

I have now been a naval architect for a good many years, designing and sailing in all sorts of vessels, including dinghies, sailing yachts, motor yachts, specialist expedition ships and sail training ships. They have all contributed one to another and it is fascinating how much cross pollination there has been between quite disparate vessels. We have been especially fortunate to be able to investigate and hopefully learn from the ships of the past. Our degree of involvement varies from vessel to vessel, from a full modern naval architectural approach to little more than a good look around. Our involvement with square rig has inevitably spilled into modern times and we have designed a number of ships for sail training. These have been particularly rewarding as we see how the challenges of sailing and the sea can affect and improve the lives of so many young people. Some of our own training ships are included, with due obeisance to the naval architects of yore, to round off this review of sailing through history.

This book concentrates mostly on sailing vessels designed in our office, but also includes one or two other ships with which we have had some involvement and which have influenced our work. There always seems to be an ever increasing amount to learn about this fascinating subject.

One more thing: throughout the book I make liberal use of the royal 'we'. The reason is that all these vessels and the various opinions put forward are very much a co-operative effort by family, colleagues, teaming partners and a very wide range of friends, and I would be quite wrong to ignore them by using the simple and imperial 'I'.

FLOATING HYPOTHESES

An approach to re-creations of ancient vessels

I should perhaps explain our office approach to reproductions, reconstructions and even 'floating hypotheses' as memorably so labelled by an eminent marine archaeologist. The greater part of our daily design work has been with sail training ships, production cruisers, commercial and racing boats. We have, I think it is fair to say, only a layman's interest in archaeology, especially in such matters as the historical associations of interesting artefacts. However, we have the designers' basic and all absorbing interest in how things actually work or worked. It is after all our daily business to make practical answers to boating problems of all kinds and to be confident enough in them to be able to wave them off to sea. Our interests are therefore principally in the practical. Perhaps our attitude to specialists is outlined in one of our office maxims, developed over many years of experience: *Only take an expert's opinion on matters of fact.* It sounds terribly rude but experts are often too close to their subject for their overall judgements to be totally reliable.

Our approach to a historical project is essentially similar to that which we use for our usual work. For any new design we spend a great deal of time, sometimes the major portion of the total time, assembling the background facts which may govern the design. In a modern vessel this may include such matters as workshop space, moulding rates, selling costs, market parameters and delivery charges before getting to the actual detail design of the craft.

For historical designs we pay particular attention to the size of the builders' community, which may determine the likelihood of the incidence of a top brain in the picture. We pay attention to their diet, which is also likely to indicate a level of technical ability. We look to see if the builders were in a port where they could and probably would share the worldwide maritime technologies. The materials available to the builder are obviously of great importance as are the sea conditions and passage making for which the ships are built. Two matters which we tend to assume are the level of craft skills and the quite different level of muscle development of craftsmen and mariners from that of our modern man. The craftsmen of antiquity were most likely to have served a very long apprenticeship before being let loose on what might be the most valuable construction in that community. Similarly, the sailing masters who operated the ships at sea could not aspire to such a position without a proper learning of their trade. Ancient man, without mechanical aids, developed, we think, a quite different order of musculature, particularly that of the upper body.

All this affects the design. We have to straddle historical accuracy with contemporary abilities. It is likely that the sailing masters of such reconstructions

As a re-creation of a 15th century caravel redonda, *Matthew* flew the cross of St George from her mainmast.
PHOTO: MAX

will be quite short in experience with ships of this kind and their unusual rigs, and so we tend to initially under-canvas the ships to give the crew some 'learning curve' time, and this may be noted in some of the plans. We also either add a discrete modern winch or put additional parts in the tackles to cater for the missing historical muscles. There may have to be slight changes in hull form to meet the modern safety regulations and possibly also to increase the additional reaction time of an untrained crew. A reproduction vessel which is going to be used amongst modern shipping also has to have an engine. The thought of her lying windless amongst dozens of twenty-knot steel ships a thousand times her size is not one to let us sleep at nights.

It is, after all, rarely possible to build with complete authenticity. The materials are different, the craft skills have probably changed and the safety authorities are on hand to bend history to their requirements. Usually we agree the maximum authenticity of appearance and performance and we discuss the authenticity of certain aspects of the construction and fit-out. For instance, it would seem perverse when building an expensive ship not to use the very best modern bolt fastenings even if they are a thousand years out of period.

Above all we believe the evidence put in front of us. Artistic licence is something of a modern invention and the historical evidence, whether painted on the surface of a vase or in the background of a painting or included in text, was put forward to a knowledgeable audience. We understand that if we cannot comprehend some aspect then we have to find why it was so and not just dismiss it out of hand. When we have developed sufficient confidence, the project goes forward in the manner usual for any modern design in our office. Lines, offsets, calculations, building plans, detail plans, specifications, sail plans, rigging schedules, etc., all follow the usual logical path and the usual office computers and electronics are employed on them to our secret amusement and satisfaction.

It is a common misunderstanding that the craft of the past were of peasant technology and that therefore the reconstructions of them can be treated without care and largely without maintenance. Despite all our best endeavours they are often maltreated after they have done their headline voyages and what is left is assumed to demonstrate that things have moved on since their day. It seems an impossible arrogance but it is all too common unless the interest and finance in the vessels can be kept up. Here I must make it crystal clear that I am not referring anywhere to the builders and expedition crews – rather those who follow.

One of the greater sadnesses about these projects is how rarely we get to acquire any direct experience in the vessels. Sometimes they are built too far away, sometimes the need to get an expedition financed and under weigh makes trials unfeasible, or as often as not we are too heavily committed to other fascinating projects by the time they are built.

We of course receive reports and in many ways these may be a better illustration of the perceived properties of vessels than a couple of days boating in the sunshine. We supply the larger vessels with a Performance Reporting Log. When the vessel is banging along in settled conditions we ask for a reading of all the instruments at that time. Seamen, however, often it seems have more important things to do than to contribute data for us. The sooner we can get the black boxes installed the sooner we shall know what they have been getting up to.

SAILING SHIPS AND YACHTS
Sailing performance in the past, and now

We often read that early man started to sea, probably only able to sail downwind until after aeons of dull thinking the crowning ability of the sailorman – to sail to windward – was achieved. This must be rubbish if you have ever tried to sail anything. The natural hydrodynamics of waterflow past even the humblest wind driven log make it luff up into the wind. Mankind's early efforts were therefore the more likely to have been attempts to make any kind of controlled sailing downwind. We can therefore assume that the invention of steering, probably no more than an afternoon's work for the thickest of early sailormen, was the mainstream from which all our historic admiralty sprang.

The history of sail appears to be littered with such misapprehensions. Many, if not most, would seem to be rooted in twentieth century yacht racing. It is difficult not to apply the criteria of contemporary yacht design to the ships of the past and very often to appear to find them wanting. Yacht racing, however, is a sport played to artificial rules. Very often the efficiencies developed for modern sailing craft are efficiencies under a sporting rule rather than those of the simple facts of life afloat.

We modern sailors used to wonder why the ships of the past seemed to get everything so wrong. Why were they built short and deep when every one of us knows perfectly well that for speed you need length? Why did they fit all those sails and all that rigging on stubby masts? We bid for the America's Cup with our best technology which turns out to be only two sails set on very high masts. Why did they not know about the value of wing type keels and why did they put up with a really rather soggy windward performance? Why was the Bermudan rig, our modern paragon, dismissed as a poor thing for distant fisher folk? Again we know that a proper seagoing yacht ought to be able to carry all its canvas up to force 5; spinnakers are ace downwind and if in doubt you ask your crew to sit along the weather edge of the boat, seaboots outboard.

Historical sailormen marched to a different drum if that is not mixing too many metaphors.

Big ships did not want keels for many reasons. They are often an obstacle to navigation and make life unduly difficult when drying out either advertently or inadvertently. The ballasted keels which we need nowadays were not required to balance the sail loadings or to right the ship if she suffered a knockdown. In history, recovery was down to the master and crew rather than the ballast which has become a legal requirement. Hulls were therefore developed to do the job we now allocate to our keels and were designed as the windward working hydrofoils. Compared with our little keels they might seem crude and clumsy but they did their stuff in a different operating regime. From being so much bigger than our current little keel wings, the speed of the waterflow over them was relatively very slow. To maximise the windward lift they were made as short as possible to maximise the relative water speed and as deep as possible to increase the aspect ratio. These big slow hydrofoils needed a comparatively large angle of attack to develop lift and this to the sailors onboard appears as 'leeway'. The necessity of promoting this lift by maximising the waterflow meant an ability to set as much sail as could be carried in light airs. Speed through the water, reducing leeway, was more effective than pinching the last few degrees of pointing up.

It might be appropriate here to pause and mention that to optimise the windward functioning of their ships the historical sailormen sailed them with much less heel than we enjoy these days. This was achieved by kiting their sails much in the manner of windsurfers.

In this great overall sweep of craft therefore the technical oddity is probably the modern yacht. It serves us for pleasure and/or sport but it is a type and form where the distortions of rating rule after rating rule have produced a pleasant, often delightful and exciting, style of novel sailing vessel. We pay heavily for many of its features both in hard cash for the high technologies of the details of the rig and the many electronics and other expensive additions. We also pay quite heavily in operational discomforts, as again witness those poor sparrows reduced to fleshy ballast perched along the weather rail of a broadly heeling hull banging along to windward.

A model of *Lord Nelson* in the wind tunnel with full sail set as part of an investigation into the wind heeling of sailing vessels. The squares are there to break up the effect of the smooth floor.
By kind permission of the Wolfson Unit MTIA, University of Southampton

GALLEYS
The 'motor-sailers' of antiquity

The motor-sailer, a vessel using both power and sail, has always been with us. That is apart from a short time at the beginning of the twentieth century when a rather splendid image appeared amongst cruising and racing of the 'purity' of sail. Very properly nobody really wanted to take that extra thirty or forty friends or 'paid hands' to row their pleasure vessels or to embark what was then a distinctly smelly and unreliable early marine engine. Times have changed and it is now distinctly odd and unseamanlike to put to sea without a quite powerful auxiliary engine. To be caught in failing winds in a twenty-knot shipping lane effects a miraculous repudiation of total purity.

The motor-sailer of history is of course the galley. Powered by ranks of men pulling at oars for propulsion, it more or less persisted for warfare in some form or other until at least the time of the Armada. By then sailing warships could sail and manoeuvre faster in any wind and crush the oars by sailing close alongside while firing guns and derision at each other.

In a simple vessel each manpower unit might be expected to produce one seventh effective horsepower and to be able to keep that up (i.e. full power) for some twenty minutes. A vessel with twenty oars, singly manned, would therefore have a power output of some three horsepower. This pace could not be kept up for longer periods of rowing and it is suggested that the same crew, working an eight-hour shift, would only be able to produce about one horsepower. Sail was therefore very important for cruising.

The design of galleys was primarily aimed at getting the maximum value from the rowing where minute differences in top speed and endurance might swing the result of battles. Two aspects were of prime importance, first that each rower had to work in an effective workplace, second that the weight and resistance of the hull was reduced to a minimum. For the former, galleys were built very lightly. Galleys were not fast and throughout the greater part of their operating speeds skin friction was a more important factor in resistance than wave-making drag. With the need to minimise weight and skin area, galley hulls were generally built with shallow saucer sections.

Galleys were not long and thin for maximum speed but to maximise the number of rowers for whom rowing 'rooms' could be provided. Rowers, incidentally, who used their upper body muscles rather than the thighs which power modern competitive oarsmen.

With such a powerful emphasis on the efficiency of the power aspect there was little that could be done towards making the hull efficient to windward. We suspect that any skipper would have tried leeboards but that these might not have been found useful with the overall weight of any craft having a full complement of rowers and their kit. So we can see that the galley used manpower for light airs, manoeuvring and warfare including some windward work. There must have been a changeover regime with some rowing and sailing together but under sail alone the polar diagram would show only reaching and running. The lack of any stability from hull form and ballast would have been easily compensated by all hands sitting up to weather or even getting on the weather rail.

The 16th century Scottish war galley *Aileach* – a re-creation of a mediaeval 'motor-sailer'.
PHOTO: MILES CLARK

MATERIALS
The basis of construction

We have, these days, a rather short list of what we believe properly constitute ship and boatbuilding materials. We can even list them as steel, aluminium, wood, concrete and plastics. In history the criteria lay with ability to be formed into something useful for the transports of the mariners. To the above list we can quickly add pottery, leather, brushwood, bamboo, fabric, animal skins and bladders, for a start. It is quite startling for a naval architect to realise how much our current ideas of hull form stem from the practicalities of building in materials we have long given up. An easy example is the manner in which many steel ships are still built on a system of framing which has its roots in holding wooden planking together against the divisive pressures of the hammered caulking process necessary to make them waterproof. In our own time we saw the early glass fibre boats moulded with a complete reproduction of the keel and framing of a wooden boat. It is probably human nature to try to reproduce the familiar but the logics involved are probably more to do with the comfort of mind of the builder rather than that of the mariner.

One can see, for instance, that pottery can be shaped to form a strong watertight vessel of considerable size. Kilning large vessels is a tricky business and one can also see that a pottery vessel would not be favourite along some rocky shores. Pottery has been used for centuries to make raft floats. Unglazed pots with their necks sealed with clay have kept many a noble foot dry. Used in pairs to keep a fisherman afloat at his work they have, with gourds and skins, provided what might be taken as minimal marine vehicles. The pressures on pottery craft would be to make them round and fat. Now that we call it ceramics and can kiln vessels of great strength and good appearance it is possible to envisage a renewal of interest in this kind of construction. Leather comes in sizeable areas and was used as bladders as a prime flotation device, singly or in groups, and was used as a sewn skin well into the twentieth century. There are no real limits to leather cladding except the availability of suitable animals, but the shape they were wrapped around had to be soft so as not to put too much strain on the leather at the stitching.

Brushwood and other longitudinal vegetation floats and can be gathered into bundles and probably formed the premier ocean-going construction for centuries. Bundles are inevitably sausage shaped and bundle craft demonstrate variations of sausage type styling subject only to keeping the ends well clear of the water to prevent soakage. The ubiquitous bamboo with its built in buoyancy chambers does not need this clearance and can be as safe at sea as what we would now see as a more conventional raft.

In the beginning and for most of history the premier material was wood. In fact it was the only material of any dimensions available to mankind until iron could be rolled into sizeable plates. A single log of decent size makes an admirable canoe. Several logs bound together make admirable rafts. We are currently rediscovering the virtues of both types of vessel. Variations of these are still to be seen around the world and some, like the Brazilian Jangada and the Indian catamarans (particularly those of Madras), are an object lesson to modern designers in many respects, especially that of fitness for purpose.

Wood has been the greatest influence on our current views on the shape of ships. Wood is long and thin and not easily bent. The development of bending techniques for wood has given us ship curves but the extent that wood can be bent is still, mentally, a limitation on our views on form.

The log canoe and its variations are not really suitable for use in cold and windy waters, especially before the invention of oilskins and thermal underwear. The efficiencies of size in commerce and war have always been apparent and the pressures on early shipbuilders were to build ships as large as possible given only trees with which to do it. The technical problems were principally those of joining one piece of tree to another and bending the planking so as to achieve a good fat commodious hull form to carry people and goods. Over no doubt thousands of years the technology of treewood and its manipulation became of a very high standard. Wood was chosen for ships when still growing; species were important and identified; tree felling was done in particular parts of the growth cycle – timber cut in autumn when the sap is down is less prone to rot. More interesting perhaps is that particular trees grown in particular soils and in particular geographical areas were highly prized. Presumably the trace elements in the soil influenced growth and material characteristics. A tree grown on a particular side of a hill would possibly develop an asymmetrical grain pattern of value to the builders. Even at the beginning of the twentieth century this technology prevailed, trees were selected in the forests and planking matched port and starboard and, for a performance hull, planked 'bottom end forward'. Nowadays our timber comes in a lorry, pre-dried, and it is difficult to tell which end of the plank was 'up'.

Notice also that if you split, or even just cut, some timbers in two the parts will spring apart, illustrating the internal tensions. If other characteristics are suitable then such timbers are likely to be highly prized for building best boats. Cut a bit of steel, or aluminium, or fibreglass or even plywood, and the parts just lie supine. Remove a plank from a new boat and it will spring back to the shape of the tree from which it came. Cut any strake from a metal or glass fibre hull and it will happily sit there keeping the identical shape it had in the hull ready to go back. Take a plank from an old wooden boat that has lost its edge of performance and it too keeps its hull bent shape.

The size of the tree can be seen as a prime limitation of the size of ships until the development of long, reliable metal fastenings. Essentially, the single tree for the keel determined the size of the ship. For light ships, clever joining

The re-creation of John Cabot's *Matthew*: offering up one of *Matthew*'s bottom planks. PHOTO: MAX

techniques allowed two or more trees to be joined longitudinally, but by and large it was a case of one keel tree to one ship. Metal fastenings were in use for centuries as plank fastenings for clincher planking but the technique of production, hammering by a blacksmith from raw iron, produced fastenings with a longitudinal grain unsuitable for fastening large timbers together. When this was overcome wooden ships grew and grew.

Iron plating was both expensive and the plates had too rough a surface to be secured watertight one to another until the rolling mills made the metal ship possible, and rolled steel plates remain the norm to this day. However, rolled plate, convenient as it is to modern construction and calculation regimes, is historically a simple and even crude approach to ships compared with that of the past and therefore ripe for improvement.

LINES PLANS
The development of shape

Throughout the following pages there are a number of lines plans. So called because an arrangement of two dimensional lines on paper is used to define the three dimensional form of each vessel. These are a modern, that is only two or three hundred year old, convention to make some formal communication of the shape of a ship to others. They were developed primarily by naval architects to instruct builders on the form the finished ship should have. They are also the basis of the ever developing calculations which are used to investigate the hydrodynamic characteristics of each vessel. These calculations, novel in history, are now so well thought of that they are probably a quasi-legal requirement for any new ship. Certainly any naval architect who said that he had not bothered with them would get extremely short shrift. Any new vessel not accompanied by a booklet of such calculations would not be allowed into commercial service no matter how satisfactory she appeared to be on trials.

Lord Nelson in drydock in Las Palmas – a modern sail training ship hull with extended keel and skeg.
PHOTO: MAX

It is often difficult for us who were brought up on lines plans from an early age to realise that they do not speak of form loud and clear to everyone. As the history of sailing ships is inevitably bound up with their shape and since we have usually recorded them with a lines plan it must be proper to put in something of a beginner's explanation. This with due apologies to any practitioners, who can give a nod to the familiar and pass on.

The lines plan is essentially a collection of cross sections of the hull form. Those which slice her up fore and aft horizontally are called both *level* and *waterlines* and those which slice her up fore and aft vertically are called *buttock lines*, as a shortened version of their proper title which is *bow and buttock lines*. Where these lines do not control or illustrate the form adequately it is usual to include some longitudinal raking cuts called *diagonals*. The disposition of all these lines results in the ability to draw vertical cross sections of the hull and these are, oddly enough, called *sections*. A formal set of these at a more or less regular spacing along the hull is used as the calculation base and when the design is calculated to everyone's satisfaction further sections can be plotted for the instruction of the builders. The so called 'offsets' for the hull form consist of a series of dimensions taken off the design board grid and which can be reproduced at full size by the yard. The word offset meaning the distance to be set off from a datum, which will usually be the hull centreline for waterline offsets and an under keel datum line for the height offsets.

The builders used to plot these out full size in their mould lofts and use them to develop the frames, bulkheads and all the parts of the ship. Templates were issued from the loft for the craftsman builders to build the individual hull components to be assembled in due course into a hull of, hopefully, close to the required form. It is only fair to say after a comment like that it is our experience that some builders are remarkably accurate, getting unbelievably as close as three millimetres overall of one hull. Others may be lucky to achieve a three hundred millimetre margin.

The traditional full size plotting is currently in decline and very often the various shapes are produced in the computer and plotted out full size by machine. Sometimes the lines are plotted at the yard to a one to ten scale but increasingly, for steel hulls, the designer's computer-generated form goes directly into metal cutting.

It is, I think, proper to note that the production of lines plans by designers is a modern convenience but can be suspect as a poorer substitute for the vessels built by eye by a master shipbuilder. The latter can, or perhaps historically could, make a much better control of the relationship between the materials and the form. With a close relationship to every aspect of the construction over what might be a period of years he would have a much better awareness of the practicalities of every detail of the construction and form.

To revert to the lines plan. It is a constant and apparently fascinating mystery to many as to how we manage to draw such a myriad of lines which apparently interlock to define a surface of at least smoothness and often beauty.

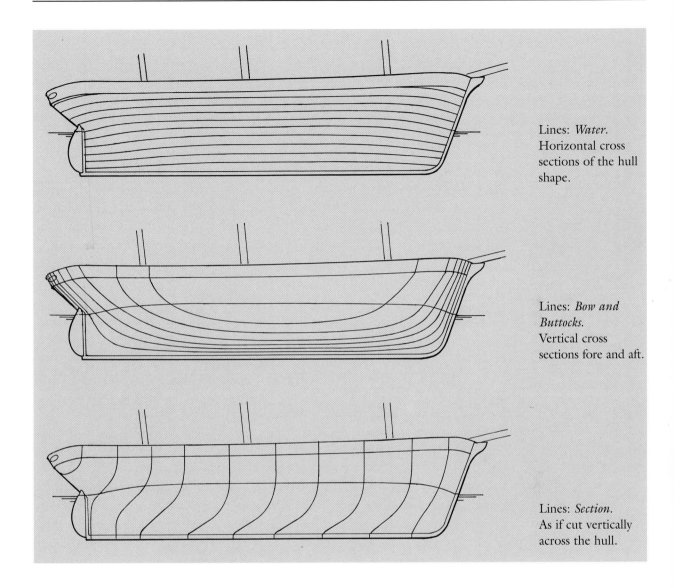

Lines: *Water.* Horizontal cross sections of the hull shape.

Lines: *Bow and Buttocks.* Vertical cross sections fore and aft.

Lines: *Section.* As if cut vertically across the hull.

Unfortunately the word seems to be around that this should be done by a process of 'fairing'. That is, adjusting each line bit by bit, one against another, until no anomalies can be detected. Computer lines drawing programs even boast that they include fairing which is very unfortunate in making this amateur approach to form appear respectable and normal. It is a shame because, traditionally, the naval architect draws a fair hull form, not fairs a hull form. We, apparently increasingly few, who know how to do it ought to get the process into our own computer programs. Take a look around the computer generated sailing boat hulls and compare them with, for instance, those of Laurent Giles and wonder why fifty years of electronic fairing has not yet caught up with him for the actual fairness of his lines plans and the beauty of his hulls.

Fairness of form is a much more easily understood concept than that of fairing. Fairness is defined in the dictionary as *'beautiful'* while fairing is *'to make smooth and regular'* and I think that says it all.

Argo

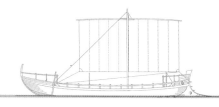

Jason's galley re-created for Tim Severin

13th Century BC & 1984

Dimensions			
Length overall		54.17 feet	16.50 metres
Waterline length		48.33 feet	14.73 metres
Beam		9.33 feet	2.84 metres
Sail area		300 square feet	27.90 square metres
Displacement (*light*)		5.63 tons	5.72 tonnes
Displacement (*loaded*)		8.09 tons	8.22 tonnes
Construction	Wood		
Rowing crew	20 places		

The Project

Of all the vessels that brought it home to us that we were dealing with some-thing of the utmost sophistication in antiquity, it was the *Argo* galley we designed for Tim Severin. So taken aback were we by the high standards that emerged from our research that we wrote to a world-renowned anthropologist about them. He told us that things were even worse than we had thought and that there was no evidence that mankind's brain ability had increased since the agrarian revolution of some seven thousand years ago. It was therefore reason-able to accept that a vessel, noted in history as being of such perfection that she must have sprung from the hand of the goddess Athene rather than from the hand of man, may have been of a high level of sophistication. In more mundane terms we realised that any vessel of some fifty-four feet in length which would have to carry more than twenty heroes with their armour, food and water, booty and captives, and have no more power than three horsepower when operating in cruise mode, had to be a bit special. The three horsepower representing the normal power produced by the rowers over extended periods. This becomes even more technically alarming when put against the Argonauts' historic armed 'trading and raiding' voyage to Colchis, some fifteen hundred miles away from home.

Direct evidence was a trifle sparse, mostly vase paintings and texts from a considerably later period. Providentially Tim Severin had unearthed a boat

OPPOSITE: *Argo*, the re-creation of a 13th century BC Greek galley, with Tim Severin at the helm.
PHOTO: JOHN EGAN/ TIM SEVERIN

Argo. Sitting or standing – the standard rowing configuration used as the basis for the design.

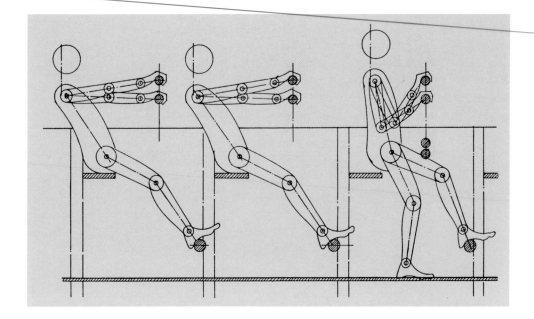

depiction on pottery from mainland Volos dated 1600 BC, Volos being the reputed building site for the original *Argo*. This gave us a span of technical illustration which helped to stabilise the style of the vessel in our minds and really gave us considerable comfort. Items with ship depictions such as these were sold when new to a knowledgeable audience and could be assumed, we thought, to be accurate in the technical details they illustrated. Another prime source was of course the *Odyssey*. It has many references to the everyday use of ships and these ships showed every sign of being close to the *Argo* galley in style and operation. Comfortingly, it also refers to the 'wisdom of the ancients' and we took this to mean that there was no feeling that the ships of the Trojan wars were in any way gross improvements on those of the past. In logic there was no real reason why they should be in that they were built from the same materials, were of the same size and powered by the same power units – that is human oarsmen and the winds.

Our terms of reference from Tim Severin were specifically for a galley of twenty oars suitable for the long voyage to Colchis and back with a Golden Fleece. This is probably the smallest size of galley of the period. Galleys of twenty, thirty and even fifty oars are reported. Homer in fact refers to the Cyclops and his great cudgel *'huge enough to be the mast of some great dark merchant-ship with its twenty oars, well used to transversing ocean's depths'* which seemed to tie in well enough as a historical confirmation that the size Tim required was quite practical for ocean voyaging.

So where do you start? Well first there is the need to provide space for the main engine – that is twenty heroes, presumably of substantial stature and ample muscle development. We followed the modern convention and gave each a 'room', as the Scandinavians call it, of three feet – that is the distance between the thwarts. Each oarsman would have to pull his weight and be able to dig his oar into his piece of sea with maximum efficiency. To our great pleasure the details on our vase illustrations seemed to show detail after detail for the benefit of the rowers. First one might notice the ram bow. There are several benefits from this but one of them is in knocking down the bow wave in way of the forward oars. The long fine entry resulting from the ram is balanced at the other end of the hull by a broad flat shallow stern. The asymmetry between the hull form fore and aft is a common device to restrict any tendency towards what might be called pendulum pitching, which is little benefit to oarsmen trying for maximum power.

Another, and possibly the most interesting, feature to the eye is the high curling sternpost. A rowed vessel can only improve its power weight ratio by adding power in the form of more rowers or reducing hull weight by a lighter construction. One of the problems of light construction is in the energy lost as the hull flexes. Properly the energy of the oarsmen has to be conveyed to the hull by their backsides, feet and the oarlocks or oarports, and from there to the underwater hull. As they power forward the underwater hull also receives energy at the bows from the water it encounters. The hull therefore can be regarded as a kind of engine receiving and delivering energy in its normal daily operation. What happens to that energy is critically important at the top end of performance. If the forward energy is returned at the bow the hull 'resistance' is increased. If it can be conveyed through the hull and returned at the stern the 'resistance' is decreased (have a go at Newton's balls on the executive desk if you have any doubts). The naval architect is interested in both the conveyance of this energy and how much is lost in hull movement. This is where the value of pre-stressing the construction is acknowledged. In our vase illustrations the high stern was, we thought, how we would use a tree as a keel, bottom end forward, with the tail pulled over and secured to provide a simple pre-stressing. One can also read into the same objectives the use of an external stem knee in that it too can be used to pre-stress.

It goes on. We read in the *Odyssey* of a feature of such ships; there would seem to be a fore and aft structure under the thwarts, called a zuga. This appeared to be of a cage form and apparently was very useful for storing booty and captives. Now a very light vessel with a considerable load of heroes and their

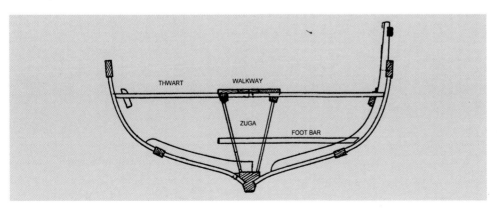

Argo. This section shows her smooth and easy form, the interlapping of the frames and floors, and where we think the mysterious zuga would have been fitted.

21

An Arthur Saluz visual of *Argo* in her Jason livery which shows the ram and the sprung stern.

gear (possibly as much as two tonnes) is potentially liable to go out of shape, especially in the form of sagging or hogging. This is always detrimental to performance. However, if the vessel was put on the beach this cage structure could be released, the hull set up again and the cage refastened. There is absolutely no evidence that we have been able to find that this was so, but it is a possibility of no more sophistication than the apparent approach to everything else in the ship.

These vessels were built with planks secured to each other with a series of tongue tenons, each morticed into the adjacent planks and secured by a tapered dowel driven from inboard. These dowels, when wet, swelled and secured the mortising, but it was therefore important that they were driven from inside the hull. It is an excellent construction for light weight and strength and for producing what was more or less a monocoque hull skin. Notice, however, that the dowels have to be driven from inboard and that the bow form is required to be quite fine. There is no place for a conventional stem knee inside the ship. Put it outboard and you have a ram bow.

We never believed that ramming was the purpose of the bow form. Sinking your enemies by ramming is not likely to be a favourite belligerent manoeuvre. Not only are you likely to lose a valuable ship which you might have conquered but you also lose booty and slaves. Also, it is not an easy manoeuvre and is likely to decimate your own forward oarsmen as you plunge in through the oars of

Argo – for full
power these
modern rowers
brace their feet
against the thwarts.
PHOTO: JOHN EGAN/
TIM SEVERIN

your opponent. This led to considering what length the ram, logical as it was, should be. We were fortunate enough to have the Yacht Design Course at the Southampton Institute adopt it as a student exercise. We tank tested different lengths and shapes and found, a little to our surprise, that the longer ram proportions (of what we had suspected were possibly rather macho vase depictions) came out best in every department.

This *Argo* was built by Vasilis Delimitros, the best shipwright in the island of Spetses, who made rather a good job of her. The Greek government gave permission for trees of Aleppo pine (pinus brutia), as used for shipbuilding in antiquity but now scarce and protected, to be cut down for her planking. The builder also cut his own 'live' oak pins, used to secure the plank tenons, from living trees. All in all constructionally she was given a very good start in life. Tim Severin and his various crews made superb voyages in her which, to us, confirmed our suspicions that in the hands of good crews these were totally first rate craft.

The Lines

The lines of a wooden vessel, especially a wooden vessel of antiquity, are usually a monument to the practicalities of construction. That is, the builder has to be able to construct the form and characteristics with the materials and craft abilities available at the building site. We are all aware that form, the solid shape of the hull, affects the performance. Perhaps we are not as aware as we might be that the characteristics of the movement of that solid shape as it responds to the energy put into it makes the difference between a good vessel and one which the goddess Pallas Athene may seem to have blessed.

However, let us look at the solid block form. A vessel of this size for rowed propulsion operates at the low end of the power curve – somewhere between half and a third of the normal maximum speed for this length of hull. At this speed the greater part of the resistance is skin friction. The builder would then have planned his hull for the minimum skin area and a skin which would be as smooth as possible. The essential hull form is rounded and smooth everywhere, given the basic requirement for a ram at the front. Minimum resistance is so much preferred by those rowing seven or eight hours a day on hard wood benches that the sideways stability is of secondary importance. In any case, like a rowing eight, a greater part of the stability is due to the oar blades themselves and beam can be reduced to a minimum to accommodate the rowers. The important need to keep the vessel in balance can be achieved by moving crew and stores.

Stability fore and aft is important in a seaway if you are to keep the bow and stroke oarsmen in effective and powerful action. It is very important in this respect to stop any pendulum pitching building up and this is dealt with by making the bow and stern quite different in character. The full fat stern form slides

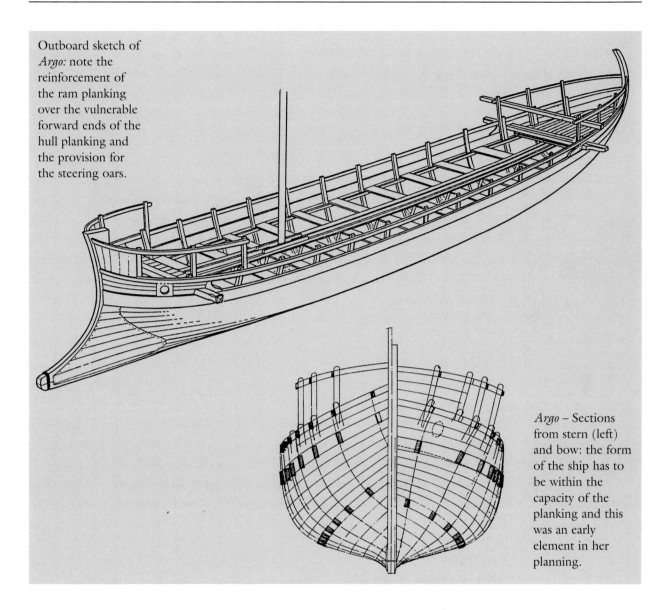

Outboard sketch of *Argo*: note the reinforcement of the ram planking over the vulnerable forward ends of the hull planking and the provision for the steering oars.

Argo – Sections from stern (left) and bow: the form of the ship has to be within the capacity of the planking and this was an early element in her planning.

easily across the water and is eminently suitable for optimising the action of the side rudders. The hull is set slightly across the flow of the water and the ram, the bow steering surface, then turns the hull.

This kind of hull pays only cursory regard to the sailing function. It may have some ability to windward in ideal conditions but this will quickly be lost when enough wind arrives to get her along. A shallow and well-rounded hull has little ability as a hydrofoil at the best of times and this will quickly disappear and she will skate to leeward if put to any strength of wind. Her squaresail should not be allowed to heel her and it may be possible for half the oarsmen to try a little motor sailing, but this would, with heavy leeway, be unlikely to please. She would, however, with her squaresail set square across the ship (not square to the wind) make good progress in, appropriately enough for the Argonauts, a soldier's wind.

Argo under sail and oars off Thassos, with different sail and black hull for the Ulysses voyage.
PHOTO: LOU LYDDON

The Voyage

In 1984 Tim Severin had the fifty-four foot galley *Argo* built in the Greek island of Spetses. After a delivery voyage to Volos, home port of the original *Argo*, he and his crew of oarsmen voyaged up the coast of Greece to pay their respects to Mount Olympus before embarking for Lemnos and the Dardanelles. After making their way up the Sea of Marmara and an epic passage up the Bosphorus, they took some five weeks along the southern shores of the Black Sea to the town of Poti, and then up the Rhioni river to their final objective – Colchis of the Golden Fleece.

Argo returned to Istanbul in a rather grander manner. She was fished out of the river by crane and returned to the coast by special train. Then she accepted a tow back to the Bosphorus by the Soviet sail training barque *Tovaritsch*. Tim also used the galley for an expedition to search for the track of the *Odyssey*, after which she was brought to England for rowing trials and preservation.

Performance

Argo powering through the Hellespont in a fair wind. PHOTO: JOHN EGAN/TIM SEVERIN

The very best guide to how the vessel behaved in practice is of course to read Tim Severin's books on her voyaging. However, some items may be abstracted.

First that with fourteen foot oars it was necessary to fit each with a seven pound counterweight to achieve a balance acceptable to a wide range of rowers. Ten men could drive her forward at about three to four knots in calm or neutral wind conditions but progress dropped off quickly with even a light head wind. The ten man manning state was apparently often used to suit a less than full complement of crew and to allow rest breaks. In good rowing conditions they would make some twenty or thirty miles in a day. On their worst day the crew rowed for a total of eleven hours.

Photographs show that for full power the oarsmen braced their legs against the thwarts in front and made considerable use of their thigh muscles in the modern manner. The original *Argo* would, we think, possibly have been considerably lighter and would have been rowed with a much greater proportion of

Argo has a ram,
sprung stern, 300
square feet of sail,
and twenty oars.

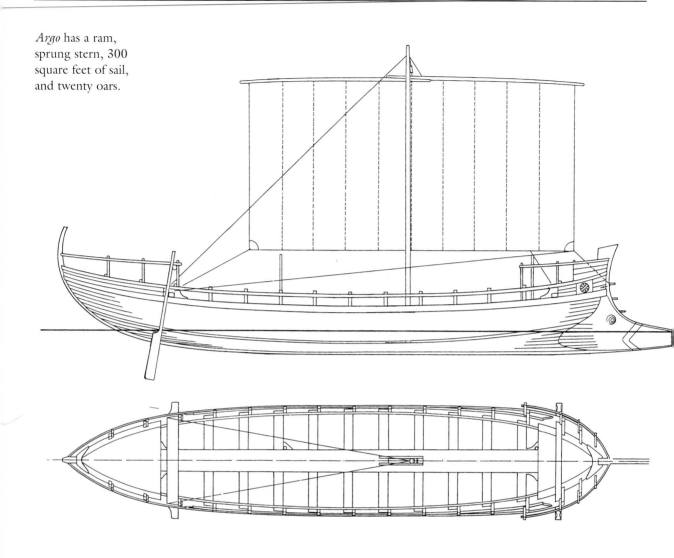

upper body strengths. She would probably, therefore, have had a slightly better
performance down the measured mile.

Athwartships trim was found to be very important, with even the slightest
angle of heel making rowing substantially more difficult. Rowing while sailing
in rough water to assist in clawing offshore was impossible due to the heavy
movement of the vessel. It was necessary to bring the oars inboard and tuck the
looms under the thwarts on the other side of the vessel to leave them ready for
use but avoid getting them caught by the seas which they feared might trip *Argo*
into capsize.

Under sail they could commonly achieve five to six knots, while on a day
reported as ideal sailing they were making seven knots. The difference between
some one hundred and fifty miles a day compared with twenty miles a day,
points to the importance of her rig and the need to work the winds to the maximum. It is not clear how high they could point under sail but it was likely to
be modest and without any effective windward component. A shallow hull starts

skating to leeward and any windward ability it possesses is stalled when there is any real force in the wind. It is interesting that it is reported that she was able to point some fifteen degrees closer to the wind after being trimmed down aft. Another point of interest is that when reaching in bad conditions they lowered the main yard a few feet to spill some of the wind from the sail and the crew lay on their thwarts with their heads to windward to add to her stability.

Manoeuvrability was said to be very good and the twin steering oars apparently worked very well although were rather vulnerable to damage. In bad weather the larger waves would slop over the gunwale and they had to pump out loose water from the bilges.

One small matter which will strike home to the heart of every oarsman: *Argo* at one stage was not slipped for ten weeks and when her hull was scraped clean a quarter of a knot was added to her performance. This may not seem much but it represents the last two miles of rowing after a hard day.

Argo was purchased out of the service for which she was built and brought to England. When we saw her next, on the Thames, someone had tarred her inside and out while she was soaking wet. The scientists and archaeologists who were trying to get data of her performance were rowing her when she was not only completely soggy but with, as far as I can remember, some half a ton of water trapped in her timbers. I do not think that our dire warnings that she should be drained of all this water within a week or so or she would rot actually struck home. Sadly, the next time we saw her she had in fact started to rot.

Hsu Fu

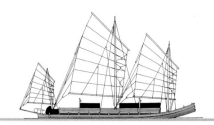

Sailing the Pacific in a bamboo raft

3rd Century BC & 1993

Dimensions			
Length		60.00 feet	12.29 metres
Beam		15.00 feet	4.57 metres
Minimum draft		1.5 feet	0.46 metres
Sail area		800 square feet	74.30 square metres
Construction	Bamboo		
Crew	5 (for the China voyage)		

The Project

The Times in 1993 labelled Tim Severin, correctly enough, as a scholar adventurer. It went on to slightly decry the archaeological values of his expeditions but to praise him as adding greatly to the gaiety of nations. Archaeologists, you see, are supposed to dig up things they can conserve and handle and on which they can make learned and possibly rather dull pronouncements. To draw your facts from the written texts of history and to cross check them with adventurous practical trials seems to me to be not just equally valid research into history but to be working on a substantially more valuable level.

The initial telephone call from Tim Severin at the start of a new project is usually an introduction to the pleasure of investigating an unusual and invariably fascinating branch of our trade as boat designers. What we understood of the *Hsu Fu* project, history apart, was that he was proposing to build a sixty foot raft of bamboo and to sail it, not just drift it, across the Pacific from Vietnam, to Hong Kong, Taiwan, Japan and then to America. His objective, we understood, was to see whether there could have been maritime contact between the Far East and the Americas two thousand odd years ago and whether this might have been achieved in the Formosan sailing rafts. Professor Needham, the great specialist in Chinese science, told him that such voyaging would be the only satisfactory explanation of cultural similarities between the high cultures of Asia and pre-Columbian America.

Hsu Fu himself, after whom the raft was named, was a Chinese navigator who was despatched eastward by the emperor Shi Huang Di (he with the terra-

OPPOSITE: *Hsu Fu*, the re-creation of a 3rd century BC Chinese bamboo raft, crossing an ocean full of 20th century shipping.
PHOTO: JOE BEYNON/ TIM SEVERIN

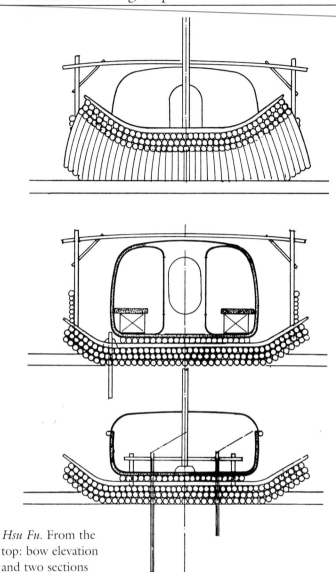

Hsu Fu. From the top: bow elevation and two sections through the cabin.

cotta warrior army) in search of life prolonging drugs. We are not certain of the outcome of this voyage – perhaps he could let us know.

Our brief was to explore the outline naval architecture of the raft so that Tim could both foresee problems in the construction and in her operation at sea. As usual his scholarship was impeccable and we were delighted with the arrival of a great deal of esoteric information. We understood that the Vietnam builders still constructing rafts for everyday fishing had not built one of this size for a very long time. The craft skills, the materials and methods of construction, were all in place but some reassurance was required to establish the main parameters.

We marked up a draft raft and then put it into our computers for assessment. A vessel composed of tiers of 150mm bamboo is not, one can say quickly, computer friendly. At least our computers of that time were not friends with the raft until we did some compromising on the intricacies of the form. We could then calculate all the usual flotation figures. Our major interest, however, was in her stability. All sailing vessels may have to face a knockdown and even a full capsize in the face of a sudden wind burst. To our slight surprise and great pleasure it would, we found, be practicable to make her self-righting by using the tops of the two accommodation cottages as buoyancy. Even a modest and short term bit of flotation from them would help. The permeable hull structure also is, it would seem, of great benefit in self-righting and we have tried, with no great success, to draw it to the attention of the designers of cross-Channel ferries.

Next, we put together some sketches of the way such a raft might be assembled and what shape it should be, and also a sail plan with an appropriate amount of canvas in the Chinese manner. Rafts of this kind use a number of centreboards for sailing. Not only can they be placed down through the bamboo more or less wherever required but with four of them on each side plus the rudders they can be raised and lowered to balance the rig. However, they can also be lifted and lowered to unbalance and thereby speed a manoeuvre.

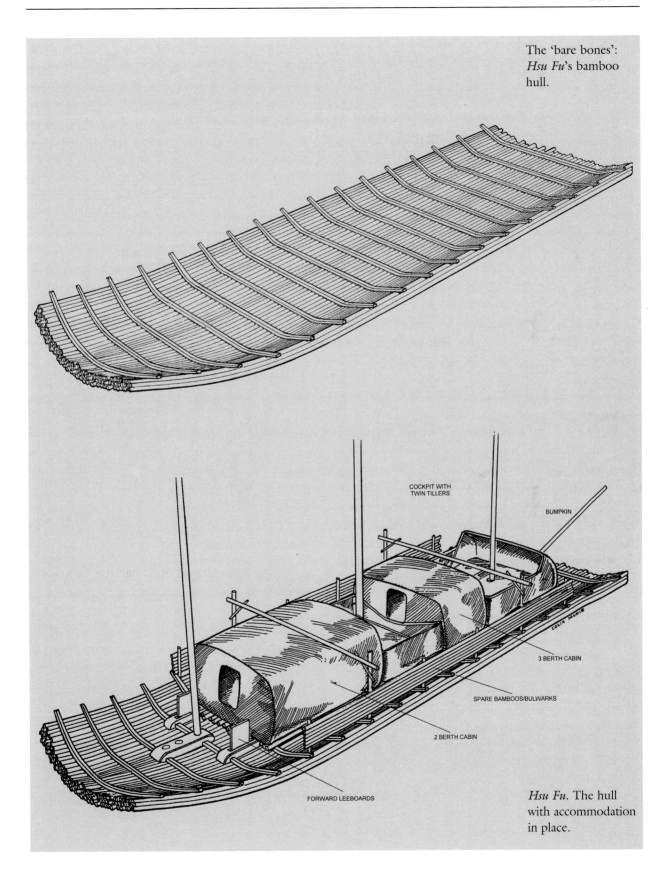

The 'bare bones': *Hsu Fu*'s bamboo hull.

COCKPIT WITH
TWIN TILLERS

BUMPKIN

3 BERTH CABIN

SPARE BAMBOOS/BULWARKS

2 BERTH CABIN

FORWARD LEEBOARDS

Hsu Fu. The hull with accommodation in place.

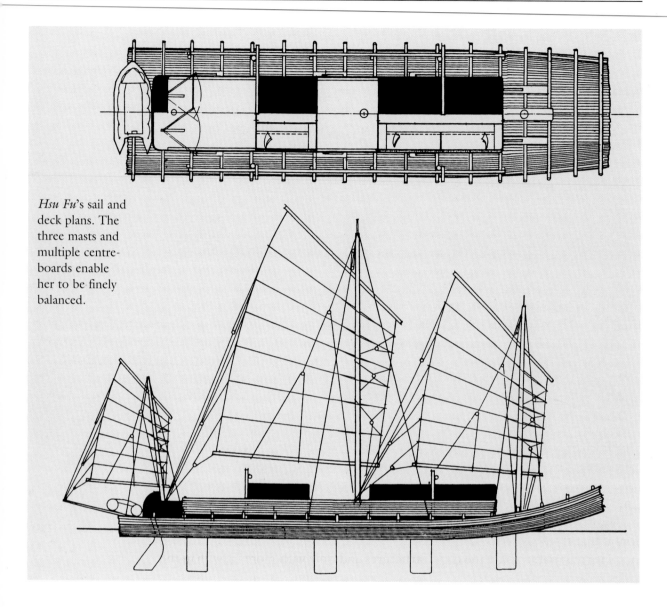

Hsu Fu's sail and deck plans. The three masts and multiple centreboards enable her to be finely balanced.

Such initial sketches form a quite practical method of communicating with the builders. They do not have the commitment of firmly drawn detailed plans but convey the general requirements for the vessel. The builders feel free to work to their usual pattern and detail and Tim has some reassurance from our work that it is likely to be along the right lines.

In any case, Tim and his team built a half-sized model of the raft in order to see and learn the building techniques and to test it to assess its safety for the expedition. By inducing comments from the local specialists this was a valuable and time saving exercise.

Two items in particular were notable. First was the need to fit some form of leaf springs, in bamboo of course, to support the raised fore end when surging into head seas. It is interesting that these should be required as leaf springs emphasising the value of flexibility as a positive virtue of the raft form. The

The Voyage

In 1993 Tim Severin built a sixty foot bamboo raft in Sam Son in Vietnam, and with a crew of four sailed some two thousand miles to Hong Kong, Taiwan and Japan before starting on the main voyage of some four thousand five hundred miles towards the coasts of North America. One hundred and five days out from Tokyo *Hsu Fu* ran into a difficult wind pattern and at the same time they found that the bamboos of the raft were beginning to come adrift. The voyage had to be abandoned. Although her crew left the raft with her sails up, sailing on and with a note on board asking for any news of her, nothing further is known.

second was more surprising in that it was made clear that *Hsu Fu* should be fitted with hogging trusses. The optimum amount of flexibility was obviously limited.

The report on the building of this half-sized *Hsu Fu* brings with it a whole range of technical terms and procedures to be savoured. Two-year-old (not three-year-old, as by then they lose flexibility) bamboos should be autumn cut when the sap is down to be clear of attack by cellulose saccharine eating larvae. They are then skinned and fire-bent (if required) to shape. The bamboos are then smeared with a shipworm barrier of toxic lacquer mixed with tung seed oil which is considered better, if more expensive, than fish fat. This latter, incidentally and surprisingly, prepared from sharks. The skins are then boiled in lime sand and used for lashings. For the full-size raft the bamboos were bound with rattan, historically coated with bitumen.

However, the main purpose of this half-sized raft was sea trials and it was found that she could sail and manoeuvre. She could be capsized and righted, but not with any water inside the cabin structures and only with more crew than the full-sized raft would support. On the positive side it was noted that a capsized raft was about as comfortable at sea as an un-capsized one and made a good survival platform.

The fact that use of seagoing rafts had persisted in Formosa from the days of Hsu Fu until comparatively recently was of course something of a comfort as to their practical ability in open waters. There were also recorded detail of their masts, sails and rigging which we could use for our own general guidance.

The masts were of straight cedar and the sails of multiple strips of coarse canvas sewn with silk and supported in the classic Chinese rig manner with between ten and twelve battens. Traditionally, the canvas was first dyed in betel juice and then in pig's blood and when dried had a dark red chocolate colour. Perhaps it is our natural delicacy which has stopped us enquiring where Tim Severin's sails acquired their red chocolate colour.

Although the current and much smaller seagoing rafts operate with a single sail we were all keen on the ocean sailors' guiding principle of at least two of everything and she has in fact three masts. We were also happy to accept the traditional Chinese rigging system for the sails. When you see how much string is involved it is perhaps surprising that we very much prefer it to other rigs for its simplicity.

We all thought that the limiting factor for the life of a bamboo raft would be in the continuous immersion of the bamboo itself. We all thought that perhaps six months might be the sell-by date. We were wrong; after six months the bamboo remained in good condition but it was the rattan bindings which rotted. Perhaps the original ocean-going rafts had bitumen-coated bindings, perhaps they had a replacement regime. Both seem eminently possible and the rotting of our rattan does not seem in any way to detract from the overall hypothesis that Tim Severin so nearly proved.

Performance

Bamboo rafts have, by ship standards, a quite excessive skin area and no one, I am sure, expects them to be fast. Her early voyaging was disappointing in terms of speed for she was only averaging about one knot. It may have been a learning curve, or the wind conditions, for she later seemed to pick up her skirts and began to average between two and four knots.

Bamboo rafts are, of course, flexible and Tim records that she moved and flexed with every sea. Her outstanding characteristic, I think confounding our apprehensions, turned out to be a quite outstanding seakindliness even in the most extreme conditions. Approaching seas charging into her open bamboo structure were just absorbed, to spill out peacefully on the other side of the raft. She stayed level throughout and Tim reported that he could stand a cup of coffee on the cockpit sole in any conditions without it slopping over. All this, I gather, with a distinctive moaning or groaning from the movement of the bamboos. In conditions which might embarrass a yacht of her size she felt, I understand, utterly comfortable and safe.

Perhaps another surprise, considering her flat-bottomed form and absence of keels and so on, was that when the sails were trimmed and the centreboards adjusted it was possible to lock the rudders, when she would run forward as if on auto-pilot. Tim, however, has expressed some concerns that the pressure on the centreboards caused them to attempt to prise apart the structure.

Amongst his other research material Tim gave us the results of some Chinese tank testing of rafts. They were looking at the possibilities of improving their speed but the results were quite fascinating and probably extremely useful to us in the future. All in all *Hsu Fu* gave us a great deal to think about.

Liburnian

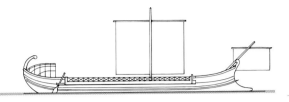

1st Century AD Roman warship

Dimensions			
Hull length		74.50 feet	22.70 metres
Beam		13.30 feet	4.00 metres
Draft		2.00 feet	0.60 metres
Sail area		456 square feet	40.50 square metres
Construction	Wood		
Rowing crew	36 places		

The liburnian was the everyday small warship of the Roman Empire. No doubt, like any so-called class of vessels which persisted over hundreds of years, there were many variations. However, when the Maryport Trust asked us to plan one for their new museum extolling the history of Maryport as a Roman base in Britain it was agreed that a twenty oared boat was likely to have been typical.

Our research, as ever, was into the purpose and normal use of such vessels as a necessary preliminary to looking into their design. Rowing galleys were the everyday stuff of ancient warfare and commerce, and the everyday design features were quite well established. The name 'liburnian' must, we thought, have some significance as it referred to the type of galleys used by the pirates of Liburnia to prey on passing craft. Pirates would, we thought, require speed and agility for the chase coupled with the ability to deliver heavily armed men to quickly board and subdue the other vessels. We could also, we thought, be certain that pirates would not want to ram and sink or set their opponents on fire, thereby making the whole piratical exercise useless. On the other hand, they might want to stand off and disable with spears and arrows.

We found that the Roman army used liburnians all over the Empire. In addition to their use as fighting craft, they were also employed for all manner of purposes including the transport of stores and horses. It is not clear whether the armies took construction kits with them but it seems likely that a liburnian could be readily built by army boatbuilders wherever there was suitable timber. It seems likely that they were used more for armed raiding and fleet supply than in any kind of line of battle. This, of course, reflecting their piratical origins.

While we were working on our research we had one of those moments of serendipity. Early for a concert at the Albert Hall, we wandered into the Victoria & Albert Museum. In the plaster cast room we found a cast of Trajan's column.

A proposal for a
Roman liburnian
with outrigger
boxes.

A proposal for a
Roman liburnian
without outriggers.

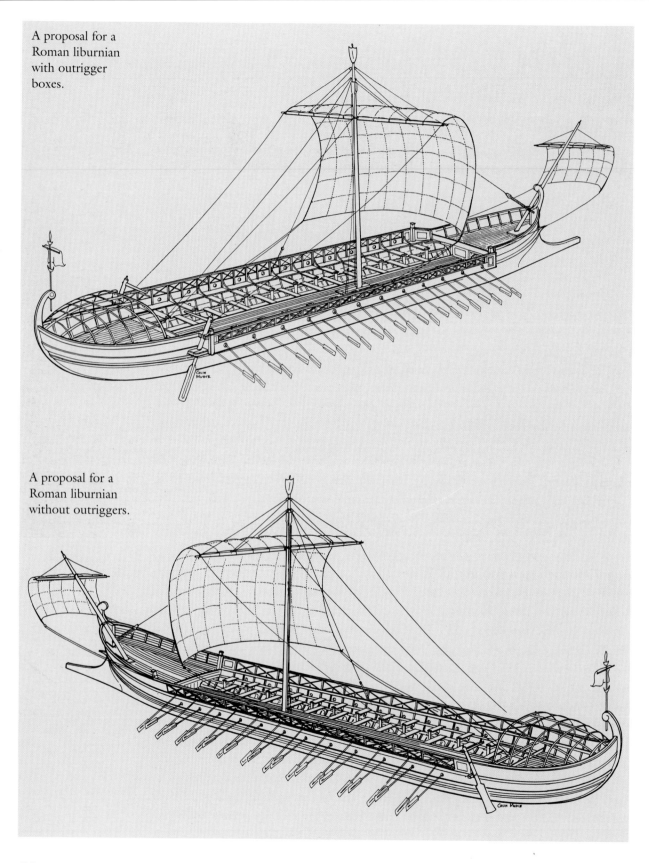

As a Victorian cast it was in much better condition than the actual column itself in Rome and depicted his campaigns with detailed carvings of the boats – the liburnians no less.

By now we were making our initial sketches and, as ever, circulated them to the academic experts for their views. Usually this is something of a dull thud, as few in academe would seem to want to trade views on practical boatbuilding and seafaring with a naval architect. However, with the liburnian we came right up against the academic buffers. Our proposals showed the use of outrigger sponsons for the oars. We had good reason for this. Not least that the Maryport Trust had engaged a researcher who found, I think it was seven, references to the use of such sponsons, which were widely known and used in antiquity. Furthermore, we could, as draftsmen, detect such sponsons on the depictions of vessels on Trajan's column.

It seemed to us that it would have been a logical feature for the original pirate craft, which would need to have had an additional turn of speed, rather

The arm musculature of Roman rowers. Detail from the plaster cast of Trajan's column in the Victoria & Albert Museum. PHOTO: MAX, REPRODUCED BY KIND PERMISSION OF THE VICTORIA & ALBERT MUSEUM

The proposal for a Roman liburnian – the practical run of planking from the bow (left) and from the stern.

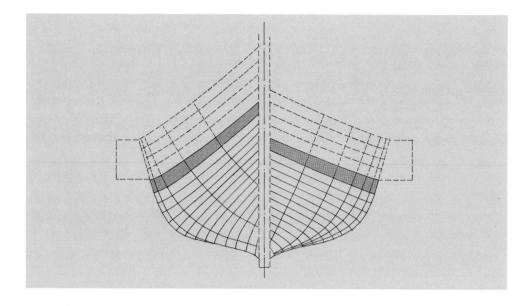

than for the Greek type of galleys, which were in common use by the non-pirates. It would also explain why the name persisted as a distinctive type of vessel for centuries.

However, we found ourselves deep in academic vituperation for holding such a view. The obloquy and scorn seemed largely to be being shot over our heads at other academics. We in the middle received letters in the same post from equally distinguished authorities saying that we were in the view of one desperately wrong and in the view of the other totally correct.

The academic battle going on around our ears produced other details, which seemed to us to be lacking in practicality. For instance, someone suggested that liburnians would have a protective cover over the oarsmen and that the fighting

The alternative rowing positions proposed for the Roman liburnian – the cause of much discussion as to whether Roman oarsmen used outriggers (left) or not (right).

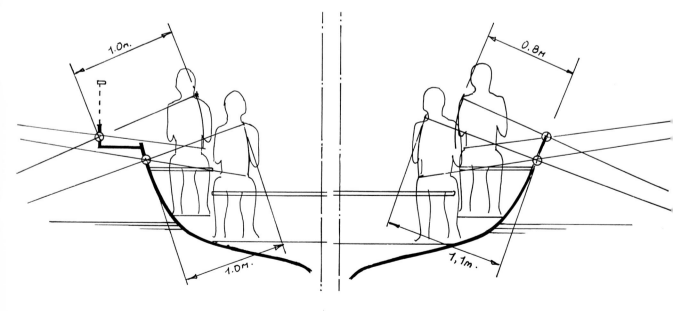

men would emerge one at a time from one end. This did not seem to gybe with any film we have ever seen about pirates. Another was that the piratical attack would involve creeping up from astern on the boat in front but that the pirates, being sportsmen, would not wish to equip themselves with an intrinsically faster boat. Incidentally we were told at the same time that the use of outrigger sponsons would result in an extra knot or so or something like an extra twenty per cent of speed. Pirates chase their prey and it did not seem likely that they would turn down such an easily achieved boost to their incomes.

Yet another source of argument lay in the style of rowing. We had been convinced that rowing in antiquity used mainly upper body strength. We had considerable grounds for this view and they were strongly reinforced by the crews of Trajan's ships as shown on his column. They were carved with enormous shoulders and arm muscles. However, this view was almost instantly dismissed in academe where it was known that the only method of rowing was thigh powered as still practised in University contests.

All this rumbled on until one and all were sick of it and the project was stood down for the time being. It was a shame because the Maryport Museum were planning to build one boat initially by the cold moulded process to demonstrate the ability of the type, followed by one built in the full traditional Roman pattern. There was some thought that this might take off into a new sport of galley racing which would be entirely suitable for the Solway Firth where if you do not row fast enough you may have to spend a tide aground on their mountainous mud.

Brendan

A leather-skinned curragh for an Atlantic crossing

6th Century AD & 1976/77

Dimensions			
Length		36.00 feet	11.00 metres
Beam		8.00 feet	2.44 metres
Sail area (without bonnets)		200 square feet	18.6 square metres
Construction	Leather-skinned framework		
Rowing crew	10 places		

The Project

Our newly joined fashionable Parisian sister-in-law, making her first visit to the London Boat Show, began, we think, to have serious reservations about her new family when we told her with some pride that the strong odour which permeated Earl's Court that year was the fragrance from one of our designer products. She may have had similar reservations about our deep need for elementary French lessons when we explained that it was in fact emanating from our '*bateau en cuire*'.

It all goes back to the sixth century AD legend of the voyaging Irish monk St. Brendan the Abbot, and comes forward again with the interest of Tim Severin in demonstrating or disproving great tranches of the history of exploration. St. Brendan, by all accounts and especially that of the *Navigatio Sancti Brendan Abbatis*, was a seafaring man who voyaged broadly about the edges of the British Isles and neighbouring Europe in the course of his saintly business. He is thought, for instance, on one voyage to have sailed to Iceland, taking forty days to do so, and then voyaged, via the Shetland Islands, back down to the Brittany coast. Obviously a well travelled and experienced seaman.

On his return to Ireland on one occasion his mother, or in fact his foster mother, advised him that some problem in the past meant that it was inadvisable at that time to linger in Ireland and that another long voyage might be appropriate. A recurring theme in early Irish folk stories is of the existence of the marvellous, beautiful and holy isle of Mag Mell, also called Tin na Og, to the westward, and St. Brendan resolved to make for it. In later versions this island assumed the name of Hy Brasil which may or may not be significant.

OPPOSITE: *Brendan* – Tim Severin's 36 foot leather-skinned curragh in which he crossed the Atlantic to verify the 6th century voyage of St. Brendan. PHOTO: NATHAN BENN/TIM SEVERIN

He put to sea again, it is thought in AD 525, and his adventures along the way included the famous and possibly fabulous picnic where he and his crew made land on a small island and went for a well-deserved run ashore. They had just lit a fire and were boiling their billies for supper when the island turned into a whale and swam away. Other adventures have a slightly greater ring of truth to them, including cross tacking with an iceberg and sailing close beside an erupting and possibly Icelandic volcano. All in fact serious confirmations that these facets of the northern route to America were well known to the writer of the text of the *Navigatio* and very nearly proof positive that St. Brendan the Navigator made such a voyage. Tim Severin was convinced at least of the value of checking whether an early mediaeval Irish boat was up to making such a serious voyage.

It is interesting to note that St. Brendan put to sea on the basis of information received and therefore he was probably not the very first to discover the New World. It seems likely, in the manner in which mariners gossip to mariners, that the tale was handed down that someone, possibly Egyptian, took the trade winds to the West Indies and South America centuries before. They would most likely have sailed north again to the coast of North America to find the fair winds to bring them home, voyaging that might easily account for the lyrical descriptions of the lands to the westward. Lyrical descriptions which match the coasts of Venezuela, the West Indies and Florida. Lyrical descriptions which do not exactly match the icebound and rocky shores of Newfoundland and Nova Scotia where St. Brendan is supposed to have made his landfalls, discovered again, with some five hundred year intervals, by the Vikings and the English.

With the prevailing south westerlies in the North Atlantic it would be logical for any clewed up sailormen starting from Ireland to get up to the northward for better winds. St. Brendan apparently took such a route and probably slipped home on a more southerly route to get the south westerlies for a fair wind back to Ireland probably more than a year later. He must have returned safely as may be inferred by the actual writing of the *Navigatio*. He may also have mentioned the hard weather boating and the less than lyrical landscapes he found because there is no record of anyone wishing to follow in his footsteps, if that is not too awful a thing to say in connection with a seafaring Abbot.

The Vessel

The *Navigatio* made it clear that the vessel used for the voyage was made of oxhides stretched over a wooden frame – a perfect description of the classical Irish skin-covered wicker boats, the subject of stories from the beginning of Irish history. It is also a description which could easily cover the curachs or curraghs still in use along the west coast of Ireland. The prime questions, therefore, to be answered lay more in detail. What were they like in mediaeval times, what

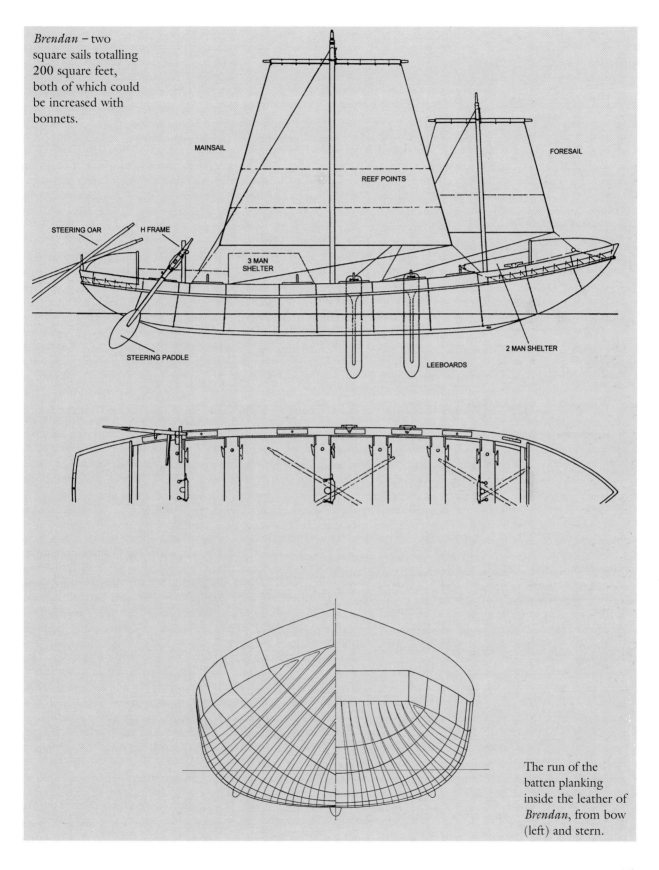

Brendan – two square sails totalling 200 square feet, both of which could be increased with bonnets.

MAINSAIL

FORESAIL

REEF POINTS

STEERING OAR

H FRAME

3 MAN SHELTER

STEERING PADDLE

2 MAN SHELTER

LEEBOARDS

The run of the batten planking inside the leather of *Brendan*, from bow (left) and stern.

size of ship would be available for this ocean work, what might be the proportions and how would it have been put together and even of what?

In one Irish story which may date to the time of Brendan, the Munster man Teigue (son of Cian) suffered a raid from some Spanish rovers and mounted an expedition for revenge and recovery. It is said that he built a great curragh with twenty-five thwarts and clad it in forty oxhides, 'hard oak bark soaked'. This ship he then fitted out for a year at sea. An elementary analysis of what might be encompassed by forty oxhides, each nominally four feet by six feet, would

The Voyage

Brendan was built at the Crosshaven Boatyard in County Cork in the south of Ireland. After launching she was taken by lorry past the Dingle Peninsula to do her early trials in the Shannon. Her voyage started officially and properly from Brandon's Creek on the Dingle Peninsula on 17th May 1976, the day after St. Brendan's feast day (a bad weather delay) and made a rather tentative way to the Aran Islands. On the next leg *Brendan* was blown well offshore and then well back again to spend a couple of days in a small harbour in Donegal.

From there it was off to Iona off the coast of Mull and to Tiree, no doubt in proper seamanlike respect for their religious affiliations. Then it was up the Minches to North Uist and Stornoway and off on the first major ocean passage: the two hundred miles to the Faeroes. Tim Severin and his crew arrived there on 24th June, just five weeks out from Brandon's Creek.

On 4th July they put to sea again on the eight hundred mile passage to Reykjavik, arriving on 16th July. There they inspected the state of the leather skin after two months afloat and found little more than an extra coat of lanolin to be required. They re-victualled and made ready for sea, but the weather had turned. After weeks of waiting, Tim decided that he must postpone the two thousand mile passage to Newfoundland until the next season. *Brendan* was laid up ashore and, being delicious to mice, properly chocked up clear of the ground and rodent-protected. Next year his crew mustered again and they embarked on 8th May with *Brendan* heavily laden for the long voyage. In early bad weather they were nearly swamped and later suffered a puncture of the leather from the ice through which they were passing. After these trials it is somewhat anticlimactic to note that they successfully 'discovered' and trod ashore on the New World at Peckford Island, near Gander, Newfoundland, on 26th June 1977 with their mission thoroughly proven with crew and craft in good order.

I would just like to add a comment on my use of the word 'discovered'. Land is always individually 'discovered' when you are at sea no matter what charts and compasses and satnavs you have to give you the expectation of it.

Brendan – the recreation of a 6th century leather boat, in the cold North Atlantic. PHOTO: NATHAN BENN/TIM SEVERIN

point towards a vessel of some sixty feet in length by six feet beam with each thwart in double occupancy. On the other hand the twenty-five thwarts on a three foot spacing adds up to some seventy-five feet. This might be achieved in a single thwart occupancy situation, inferring an overall length greater than a hundred feet against a beam of some four feet, which would be entirely against the received wisdom for vessel proportions and the practicalities of construction. However you look at it, Teigue was building a sizeable and notable vessel of dimensions which made the constructional style of the modern curraghs unlikely. More likely is that she was quite stoutly built in timber, possibly in the manner of wickerwork or even close planked. It would then be natural to make her waterproof with a skin of the oak bark tanned oxhides which were an integral part of the current boatbuilding technology.

We rather thought that Brendan's ship for his voyage to fair Mag Mell was likely to be a wooden ship of this kind, leather skinned, but we accepted that if the new voyage was properly to authenticate the old then it would best be demonstrated in a seagoing curragh. Brendan had after all been halfway to Iceland in a curragh, and knowing how conservative seamen are in the matter of their craft it was a distinct possibility that a curragh would again have been his choice.

The next natural question might pose an enquiry as to why Tim Severin would come to a Scotchman living in southern England for the design of an Irish craft of a type still under construction in that country. Frankly we did not linger much on that question and assumed, I think correctly, that modern curraghs were not built large enough for Tim's requirements and also that they were no longer clad in oxhides. Our design function was to look astern and do the calculations without which modern craft do not exist.

We started by casting an eye over the many variations of the curragh and quite quickly came to the conclusion that those of the Dingle Peninsula met most of our criteria. It may have been that they were pleasing to the eye in their form, and that may have been because they most nearly approached the shapes to which we were accustomed in fully wood-planked boats. In addition they had a smooth curving sheer, unlike many of the other types which had what can only be called a broken sheerline. The smooth curves giving promise of a smooth flexing without undue stress points building up in a seaway. Again, they were built on the basis of a very simple and strong double gunwale which took care of the loads of stretching the oxhides.

The rest of the naval architecture, flotation, sail areas, etc., was straightforward, with the devil in the cladding. Tim Severin researched the supply of hides, the method of tanning them and the manner in which they were sewn and greased. We, however, did some private checking of the results. We stretched various samples of oxhide in wooden frames and coated them in various recommended unguents before tossing them over the edge of the local pier. We thought that if they lasted for three months under water, free of deterioration or crab bites or other marine hazards, we could be confident that Tim would be secure for each leg of his voyage. Our fortnightly trips to inspect our smelly samples were noted with some interest along the pier. All our test pieces survived this simple trial, to our relief and satisfaction.

We also took other precautions. We insisted that the craft should be self-buoyant so that the boat and crew would remain fully afloat should the skin suffer a rip. This we did with polystyrene blocks, which I think were also clad in leather to continue the authentic theme. We could not persuade Tim or his crew that modern Bermudan sailormen would have to learn how to sail their mediaeval craft with its mediaeval rig. We suggested that they bought an old Admiralty whaler to practise with, but all to no avail. So we cut the sail area to about a one-reef rig to give them more time to respond and you will see in the pictures that, after their learning curves, they fitted bonnets.

The difficult part of the work at this stage all fell to Tim Severin, who not only had to acquire suitable oxhides but to find how they should be tanned. Oak bark tanning of leather, the traditional process, involves soaking the oxhide in

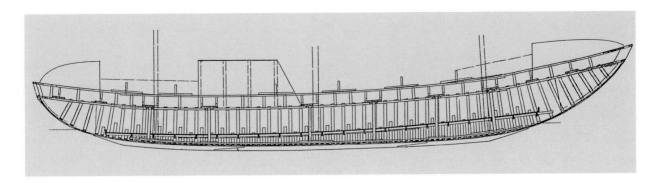

Brendan's 'skeleton', with two heavy structural gunwales and light batten framing. The third 'mast' is for the radio aerial.

ground up oak bark and water for a long period while the skin soaks up the tannin to turn it into first class leather. Even then for use as a boat skin each hide must be free from natural or man-made defects. Our simple requirement for fifty-seven of them was therefore a major problem, not made particularly easier or more simple by the follow-up process. Each hide had to be suspended in hot wool grease and the resulting stack of leather hides had, I understand, a quite notable olfactory effect for several miles around.

Performance

Tim Severin carried out proper rowing trials using fully experienced modern rowers. At full power ten men, her full complement, could achieve some five miles per hour and maintain over three miles an hour for continuous cruising. At a standard for experienced rowers that they can develop one-sixth of an effective horsepower when at full power, this is the equivalent of a four horsepower outboard motor, which is a little depressing in its way. However, from our point of view, as these trials were made *after* the ocean voyaging it would seem to indicate that the hull had not gone soggy. On the other hand we perhaps should look more closely into the performance values of the lanolin with which she was coated.

Interestingly enough, a six-man crew could maintain close to the same speed for cruising. With four men, however (her actual voyaging crew), performance fell off badly and they could not make against a current of less than one and a half knots in the sheltered waters of the Charles River in Boston. In practice they found it impossible to row *Brendan* upwind and had to take the utmost care not to be caught on a lee shore with a strong breeze.

Under sail a small shallow boat has only the most modest chance of deploying an effective hull hydrofoil for windward work. It might be expected to skate across the ocean to its benefit in the downwind direction but to slide sideways when put to windward. Such a hull needs help and the traditional aids are centre or leeboards and deep rudders. Centreboards would seem to be impractical for a leather-skinned boat and there are no discernible references to the use of leeboards on curraghs. What is more, the proportions of her side rudders make them tricky at the very least as a windward lifting agent. We have always found it difficult to believe that seamen in such a craft would just sit with their fingers in their mouths as they were driven sideways onto the rocks. It would be the most natural thing to try using the oars as resistance, and on the lee side they would quickly emulate the leeboard. There are two problems with the concept. First, that the timber available would not allow the easy construction of lee-boards of a decent fore and aft span. Second, that a narrow leeboard is the trickiest thing to set right. It, like a modern slim-keeled yacht, would have to be set to find its 'groove' and even then would probably not have the boat speed to be effective. Nonetheless we planned a set of leeboards for her, cut from single planks and with lanyards just to hook over the oar thole pins. They were found to reduce leeway, their function, by about ten degrees in normal sailing. Interestingly enough the crew removed them at wind speeds of over force 5 because they tended to scoop too much water into the boat. Sitting at my desk at least half a mile away from any force 5 at sea it is easy to think that they would only scoop water in if they were set at the wrong angle. That is, that they had negative rather than positive incidence to the waterflow.

Brendan's best day's run was one hundred and fifteen miles and her average sailing day was about forty miles. Tim has noted that in force 3-4 she would make some two to three knots, whereas in force 5-6 she could make five to seven knots. He also mentioned that his speedometer scale stopped at twelve knots and that this speed was achieved 'comparatively frequently in heavy weather and heavy seas'. To windward they could usually point the squaresail fifty to sixty degrees off the wind but making horrendous leeway of about thirty degrees.

In bad weather she seemed to have behaved well and in the worst conditions they ran off downwind under the little foresail streaming warps and spreading whale oil, which may have been a delicate tribute to the voyage of their predecessor, St. Brendan the Abbot.

Brendan, her duty done, now lives in a glass shed some five miles from the Shannon estuary and ten from the airport. Something of an Irish icon, she is to be found at the Craggaunown Project, Shannon Heritage, The Living Past, Sixmilebridge, County Clare, Ireland.

Sutton Hoo

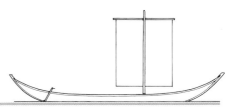

The 7th Century AD ship from a Suffolk barrow

Dimensions

Length overall	88.00 feet	26.80 metres
Beam	14.00 feet	4.25 metres
Construction	Wood	
Rowing crew	40 places	

In the middle of 1973 we were asked by Rupert Bruce-Mitford, then Keeper of Mediaeval and Later Antiquities at the British Museum, to have a shot at drawing a lines plan for the Sutton Hoo ship.

The traces of a ship were discovered when a barrow was opened at Sutton Hoo near Woodbridge in Suffolk in 1939. It was partly excavated and then closed for the period of the war and re-excavated in 1966. There were all manner of treasures found but the greatest one must be the traces of this magnificent

Dr. Edwin Gifford in his small version of the Sutton Hoo ship. PHOTO: MAX

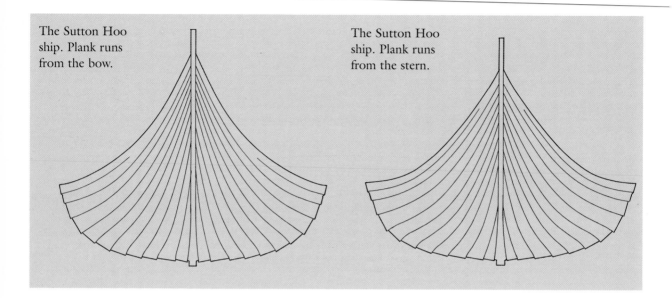

The Sutton Hoo ship. Plank runs from the bow.

The Sutton Hoo ship. Plank runs from the stern.

ship of the seventh century. These consisted of little more than the stain traces left in the burial mound from the timbers but with a complete set of the iron rivets and bolts with which she had been built and all still outlining the shape of every plank. The hull space was excavated to reveal this construction and planking, and every detail, of course, recorded. Our task, which we gladly accepted, was to draw up a lines plan for the ship from this data.

The Vessel

She was a vessel of some size – a great open boat of about twenty-seven metres in length and with a beam of 4.25 metres as found. Her depth amidships was about 1.37 metres and at the ends she measured some 3.8 metres above the keel. She was thought to draw about 0.6 metres of water and was believed to have been manned by forty oarsmen. Forty men can deliver some six effective horsepower, the equivalent of a twelve horsepower engine at full power, and for a quite short span. For cruising they would have a power output for this twenty-seven metre vessel of something like a four horsepower Seagull outboard motor, which makes one think a bit. Each rower would have required a fore and aft room of just over 0.9 metres, and at twenty per side this would have taken up 18.3 metres. Again, if they were working with oars of about 4.3 metres long, they would have required an athwartships width each of about 1.3 metres, leaving a rather spacious 1.6 metres in between them. This leads to something of a quandary about her use. She was too heavily manned to be a cargo carrier and possibly too large and bulky to be a fast despatch or raiding craft.

The solution, of course, springs from the ground in which she was found. She would have been ideal for Royal use as a flagship and ceremonial barge, and a first choice for a personal ship in which to cast off for Valhalla. Although no

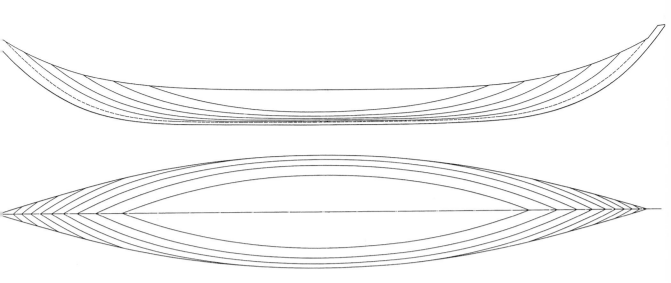

traces of his corpse remained to be found in the ship it is thought that this was the funeral ship of one Raedwald. He was one of the first kings, or Wuffingas as they were called, of East Anglia. Raedwald was apparently an early convert to Christianity but in the comfortable manners of the period apparently thought that in his funeral he might bet both ways and go fully prepared for whatever afterlife turned up.

For our part our first concern was to see if the ship had been distorted in the burial process or in the twelve hundred years she had lain underground. We could not see any sign of this and really I suppose we did not expect it. If you treasure your boats and are burying one for the afterlife of your king he would not thank you when you met up again in that afterlife if she had been spoilt. The whole lines fell in sweetly and were completely typical, and practical, clincher boatbuilding. The ends of the planks could be well supported as she was built, and the plank scarphs were equally well supported by the adjacent planking. As interesting as anything was that our lines gave her a centre of buoyancy forward of amidships. In the 1970s this might have been thought a little novel but we know now that it is correct to withstand the nose diving plunge of a hull as forty heroes bend to their oars.

Our friend Dr. Edwin Gifford has made a half model of the Sutton Hoo ship from these lines and can often be seen subjecting himself and his crew to Saxon boating at maritime events along the South Coast. He gives us a cheerful wave when we see him boating in his half model – at least we think that it is a cheerful wave, but it might just be a careful historic reconstruction of some appropriate Saxon gesture.

Sohar

Sindbad's dhow

9th Century AD & 1980/81

Dimensions			
Hull length		80.00 feet	24.38 metres
Waterline length		63.00 feet	19.20 metres
Keel		52.00 feet	15.85 metres
Beam		20.00 feet	6.10 metres
Draft		6.00 feet	1.83 metres
Sail area		2,900 square feet	270 square metres
Construction	Wood		
Crew	15–20		

The Project

In 1980 Tim Severin came to us with a project for a vessel in which to investigate Sindbad's legendary voyages. Sindbad himself is now such a pantomime figure that it takes a Tim Severin to see that the legend probably stems from a proper historic figure who undertook such a notable voyage that his adventures have been the stuff of storybooks ever since. The ship we were asked to plan for his reconstruction of the voyage to China and back had to be a suitably authentic ship of the eighth or ninth century. However, there was not a single hard fact available to guide us. Tim, as ever, had done a great deal of research and thought that she would have been a boom – a two-masted double-ended vessel extensively used for seagoing by Arabian seamen. Furthermore he had also researched the important fact that the biggest timber which would have been available for her keel would have been about fifty feet. We assumed that Sindbad, bound away on an important trading voyage, would have the biggest kind of ship and one of proven seaworthiness.

With the general type and her general size more or less settled, the question of the hull form remained. First we looked at what a ship owner, in the very nature of ship owners, would have required from his builder to suit the changing patterns of trade over the centuries. We thought that, compared with the period of Sindbad, the modern operators of dhows had fallen on comparatively hard times. High value/low volume cargoes now inevitably travel by steamer

OPPOSITE: Tim Severin's Arab boom *Sohar* (named after Sindbad's birthplace) in which he traced the voyages of Sindbad. PHOTO: RICHARD GREENHILL/ TIM SEVERIN

and even by air, as does the passenger trade. The cargoes available in the latter half of the twentieth century would inevitably be low value/high bulk in style and the dhow owners would be pressing the builders for more hull volume even at the cost of speed. By reversing this process we could make a reasonable guess that the typical ninth century boom would be a leaner and faster vessel than the many modern booms which can still be seen in considerable numbers.

Another important factor was likely to be the change in construction methods since the days of Sindbad. Early dhows were of so called sewn construction where the planks and the framing are held together by a form of sewing with rope fibres. Essentially, such a construction requires a minimum of interplank stresses and this again pointed us towards the leaner and faster vessel. The advent of iron-nailed construction would have the prime benefit for later builders and owners in securing the planking around the sharper curves of more portly hull forms.

Over all, we were a little concerned about Tim's intentions to emulate the voyages of Sindbad. We knew of Tim's search for accuracy in these matters. We were also aware that each one of Sindbad's voyages had ended with him being shipwrecked or cast away, which cast a minor pall over our original enthusiasms. Tim, however, appeared ready to forgo his exploration of the traditional folk tales to that extent. In due course the project was sponsored and underwritten by the Omani government as an illustration of the golden age of Omani seafaring from the eighth to the eleventh century and we were satisfied that this would encourage Tim to abandon any lingering thoughts about shipwrecks and strandings.

The coasts of Araby are full of dhow designers and builders, possibly as many as a hundred working yards building them today. It seemed unlikely that we could tell them anything about booms and that we could and should be able to learn a lot from them. We approached this on two separate tacks. First we made a kipper model of the initial lines and Tim took this to Oman for comments and suggestions from local builders. The advantage of a kipper model, which is an unplanked simple assembly of the hull profile and sections, is that the various views on form could simply be marked on the white plastic. This, we think, was very successful. In general the form was accepted but with a slightly greater tuck into the garboards, in fact a deeper curve down to the keel. Our view that the sternpost would have been more upright than those of modern dhows was generally rejected. Both items reflected severely practical aspects of wooden shipbuilding. It would go against the grain not to rake the sternpost to achieve the optimum size of ship from a really valuable keel timber. Again, the suggestion of a greater tuck into the garboards reflected the practical view that by doing so you can quite considerably reduce both the size of timber required for these planks next to the keel but also the work required to shape them.

Our other approach was to draw a number of sketches of details, particularly the construction, sewn seaming and the steering. Tim took these around the Omani specialists for their views. From this we were able to make a quite general approach to scantlings and from that to the estimates of weights and from

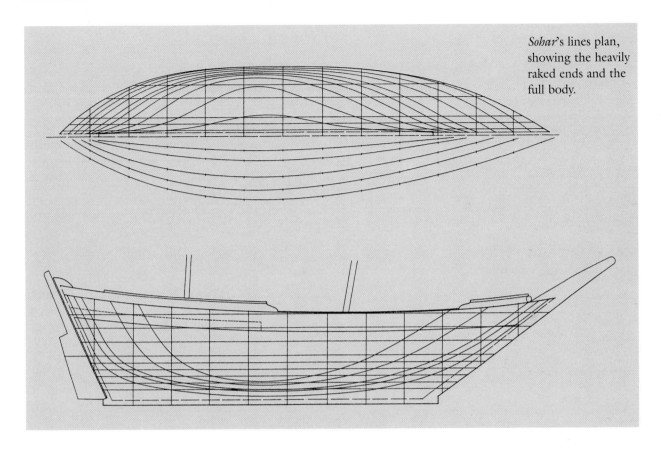

Sohar's lines plan, showing the heavily raked ends and the full body.

that to look closely at the potential stability. We drew up a final lines plan and sail plan and rather outline details of the main construction items. It would have been a quite major impertinence to have tried to instruct dhow builders on how dhows are built.

We specified washed stone or gravel for ballast but Tim very properly thought to fall in with local best practice. Sand was brought from the prehistoric Magan copper workings, it being understood that the copper content made for heavier sand to the benefit of the general stability of the vessel. A feature of which we were not aware was that it had the most horrendous smell and fumes strong enough to corrode metal.

The ship was built on the beach at Sohar and duly did her stuff with a voyage to Canton and back, and a sister ship has, we think, been built in China as an additional commemoration of both the outstanding voyage of Sindbad and its outstanding replication by Severin.

The ship herself is on display in Oman. It has been most cleverly presented. The vessel, fully rigged and maintained, lives in a close fitting dry tank which is in the middle of a shallow pond in the middle of a roundabout in a dual carriageway. On high days and holidays and when VIPs are in town the ship is manned, flags flying, depowered sails are set and water jets powered up to simulate bow and stern waves. It really is the most astonishing and attention-grabbing sight. There you are driving down the motorway when suddenly a large dhow is

Sohar, November 1980: departing Muscat, Sultanate of Oman, at the start of her Sindbad voyage to China. PHOTO: LOU LYDDON

apparently sailing across your bows. Sometimes you can meet a sailing vessel in a like manner as you drive around the Norfolk Broads but not a great ocean-going, lateen-rigged and apparently fast-moving sailing ship.

Construction

There would seem to have been some academic doubts that the double-ended boom was in existence as early as the times of Sindbad. Fortunately, Tim Severin was able to prove early existence thanks to the Portuguese mapmakers who had the delightful habit of illustrating their charts with small pictures of ships. We had little doubt that the double-ended form was likely. The practicalities of securing and making the plank endings watertight are effectively the same at both ends of the ship. There is little case, in sewn construction, for a transom stern until the ship is large enough, like the later baghlas, for any watertight problems caused by the right angle joint between planking and transom to be well clear above normal waterlines.

There are no indigenous trees in Oman suitable for building ships of this size and the timber has to be imported. That brought in for *Sohar* came, as is the tradition, from the Malabar coast of India and consisted of aini and poon. The former, for the hull, is a teak-like timber with lime in its fibres. It does not take paint easily but is as good as teak and possibly better at resisting the toredo worm. With this timber came a team of Indian craftsmen to augment the numbers of Omani boatbuilders who were available for the work.

It is notable that excellent ships are built where wood is a valuable import and not commonplace. Stitched or sewn construction requires quite outstanding craftsmanship. The hull has to be built as a shell to allow the clear run for the sewing and padding of each seam from one end of the ship to the other. Again the seams are not caulked and have to be close fitted plank-to-plank for the full length of the ship. Tim noted that they checked the fit by applying blue powder to the seam face of each new plank as it was tried up in place. If the powder could be seen to have contacted and marked the full length of the previous plank the fit was considered acceptable. Incidentally, this is a technique we use these days for metal-to-metal joints rather than for woodwork. A full-length roll of coconut fibre is then set along the interior face and included in the stitching of plank-to-plank by a complex pattern of coconut fibre lashing.

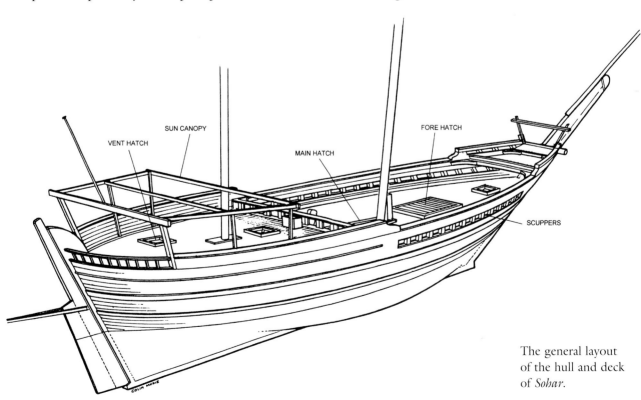

The general layout of the hull and deck of *Sohar*.

There are various views of the advantages of this kind of construction. An Arab view is that a sewn hull can more easily withstand the shocks of grounding, especially accidental groundings on coral. On the other hand it was thought that the stitching could not take the strain of gunfire. Possibly it was not so much a question of the stitching bursting but more that any cutting of the fibre might lead to a disastrous un-ravelling. Personally I have always enjoyed the logic of the view that the great magnet at the bottom of the sea would pull any iron nails straight out.

Some 140 tons of timber was cut in India for *Sohar* including her 52 foot keel and 400 miles of coconut fibre imported from the Laccadive Islands where the technology or technique for ship sewing is still available. Her bottom was coated with a mixture of lime and mutton fat and her topsides 'varnished' with vegetable oil.

Walk Through

Our original layout for the ship envisaged a crew of about ten. In fact she put to sea with about twice that number. The interior, therefore, was largely taken up with two tiers of berths against the shipside port and starboard. The Captain had his own compartment right aft with an astern-facing chart table and the forepeak, as ever, became the bosun's store. Most of the daily ship life was on deck for more reasons than one (see below).

She was launched with some fifteen tons of shingle ballast, hopefully washed as specified. In short order she developed a staggering smell of rotten eggs – hydrogen sulphide strong enough to corrode fine metal. They changed the ballast for new, clean and washed, shingle in Calicut but the rotten eggs persisted. It may just be that the original shingle was polluted but there was an interesting acceptance of the smell by the elder dhow sailors. There was an inference that this was one by-product of using coconut fibres and just a possibility that it might be connected with the particular timber used for the construction. However Tim notes with some glee that this particular environment 'is de rigeur in Indonesian vessels – odeur de bilge'.

Performance

I suppose that it is a satisfactory element of performance to report that Tim Severin, *Sohar* and a crew of about twenty, made a seven and a half month voyage and reported the vessel to be in good order on arrival in China. Over some 6,000 miles they encountered weather fair and foul and amongst other matters proved that an eighty foot boom could have traded with China at the time of Sindbad. This is possibly more of a feat than might appear since at the beginning of this century one Arab ship in ten was lost when crossing the Indian

The Sindbad Voyage

Sohar sailed from Muscat on 23rd November 1980 (Oman National day) and made her way south-westerly across the Indian Ocean to arrive at Calicut a month later where she was careened and fitted with stronger sails. From there she sailed to the south of Sri Lanka to arrive late in January. She put to sea again about a month later to spend a frustrating time with a long period of windless doldrums. They reached Sumatra in the middle of April, put to sea again early in May and reached Singapore at the beginning of June. From mid June they took the south-west monsoon winds up the China Sea to Hong Kong and then on to Canton for an official reception on 11th July 1981.

Sohar under full sail during her seven and a half month voyage from Oman to China. PHOTO: RICHARD GREENHILL/ TIM SEVERIN

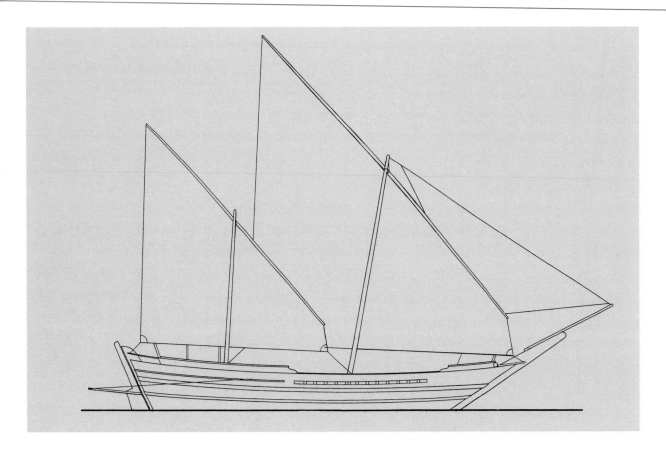

Sohar's sail plan – with lateen sails of a size usual to Western eyes.

Ocean. There was also a European view that the sewn construction, perhaps because of its novelty, was not suitable for the strains of ocean crossings. The only weak point Tim reported was that the seam between garboard and keel seeped a little. Nowhere else did she leak.

Her reported performance indicates a best day's run of some 130 miles – some five and a half knots. The maximum to which she was driven was eight or nine knots and with calms and gales she just about matched the traditional two knots or fifty miles a day used for voyage planning. With her lateen rig she could point high to about forty-five degrees off the wind but she made a disappointing amount of leeway when doing so, making good about sixty-five degrees. This leeway was unexpected and may be due to trying to optimise the way she pointed up rather than the hull speed through the water. In other words they may have been tending the rig component of windward work rather than the equally important hull component for this shape of hull. They would not have been helped of course by *Sohar*, without cargo, floating lighter in the water than the fully laden hulls of commercial sail.

Matthew

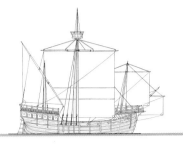

John Cabot's ship for his Newfoundland voyage

1497 & 1997

Dimensions			
Sparred length		83.00 feet	25.20 metres
Structural length		73.00 feet	22.30 metres
Hull length		63.92 feet	19.50 metres
Waterline length		61.50 feet	18.70 metres
Beam		20.50 feet	6.20 metres
Draft		6.00 feet	1.60 metres
Sail area		2,360 square feet	219 square metres
Construction	Wood		
Crew	19 (Bristol to Newfoundland)		

The Project

In 1992 I went to Bristol to discuss with the Bristol Initiative, a civic body, the design of a reconstruction of Bristol's most famous ship, *Matthew*. World famous that is, for Bristol has built many well known ships including of course the steamer *S.S. Great Britain*. The little ship *Matthew* sailed from Bristol under the command of John Cabot in the year 1497 bound for Japan via the New World recently discovered by his friend Christopher Columbus in 1492. Diplomacy and high politics required that he did not trespass to the south and so John Cabot went northabout. His instructions from King Henry VII specifically enjoined him to go by the *'backside of Groenland'*. By the time he returned he had planted the English flag on the American mainland, or at least on Newfoundland, and started the process of English sea power and expansion which led to the full panoply of the British Empire. Equally as important, he started the export of the English language which has spread to be the principal communication tongue of much of the world.

A few but significant facts are known about Cabot's ship. She was apparently of fifty tuns capacity, sailed from Bristol to Newfoundland in thirty-four days and the passage back to her Ushant landfall took fourteen. She had a crew of eighteen or nineteen, including it is said 'fourteen hearty Bristol seamen'.

The Bristol Initiative looked to build an accurate vessel of the period such as

Cabot might have employed and to sail it to his New World landfall. Their objectives were to remind the world of Bristol and to celebrate a continuing friendship with Newfoundland. Also, as we are now fully aware, they were no doubt looking forward to the kind of parties which were spawned by the project and celebrated by the people of Bristol in what can only be described as a typically hearty manner. Bristol is known for its sherry but our *Matthew* seemed to regard champagne as natural an element as good salt water.

In addition to the direct historical facts about the ship and the voyage there are a number of other facts which help to define her. She must have been built with the technology of the period which can be summarised as first rate for the wood and second rate for metal fastenings. She sailed from Bristol, which implied a good windward ability to get out of the Bristol Channel against the prevailing south westerlies. Furthermore, a Bristol Channel ship needed the largest possible sail area to make her way over the tide amongst the banks and needed to be able to take the ground with ease and confidence when she could not do so. Last but not least is that John Cabot was an experienced sailor with a Royal Charter tucked in his belt. He would have had the experience and the backing to have the very best of vessels. He also named the ship after his wife Mattea which must imply that both were high in his opinion.

A main item to settle early in the design process was her rig. Caravels of the period sported a range of rigs of which the most common were the multi-masted lateen (*caravela latina*) or the multi-masted square rig (*caravela redondo*). This took scarcely any time to resolve. A crew of eighteen might be able to handle the lateen rig but it would be hard graft and not allow for the potential losses of crew in a world voyage to Japan. Everything pointed towards the square rig. It set more canvas for light airs and produced more hull speed to reduce leeway even if it did not point so high as a lateen. The actual sails are not so large as the lateen and easier to handle by fewer crew. The balanced sails meant that most sail adjustments and even some manoeuvres could be carried out without calling the watch asleep below. Possibly most important to the experienced explorer is the ability of the square rigger to stop and twist and turn and even sail backwards. Imagine the comfort of such ability when standing in to a strange coast on a misty morning.

Her overall size was quite well defined by her known ability to embark fifty tuns of wine. Shortly afterwards a formula was established to define this capacity without having to resort to physical tests and we thought ourselves safe to use it to establish some likely main dimensions. We were also aware of certain historical proportions for this kind of ship and in any case all our conclusions would eventually be fed into our computers for a final check that we were on the path for a good seakindly vessel. Any conclusion that pointed towards anything other than a fully seaworthy vessel would obviously have been totally wrong.

Everything else fell equally sweetly into place. We pondered a bit over the illustrations which showed the tiller of the rudder disappearing into quite heavy

OPPOSITE: *Matthew*
PHOTO: MAX

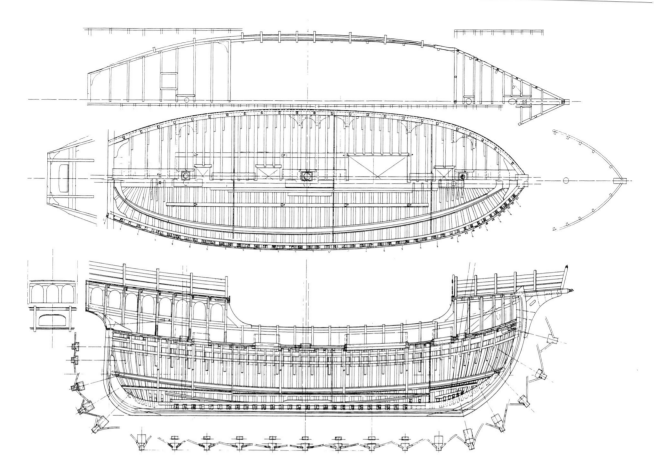

Mathew's construction plan. The ring of sections outside the hull plot the detail of the main centreline construction.

poop decks with the helmsman apparently doing his stuff without sight of the sails – which seemed unlikely. We could find no trace of whipstaffs or even steering wheels which were common in later years. The answer was best illustrated by contemporary illustrations of earlier craft. They had poop decks over the helm but they were open sided so that the helmsman was fully in touch with all that was going on. This approach seemed to fit well with the habits of the seamen we know to this day. The poop deck of a *Matthew* was there for two reasons. First, to keep the rain and spray off the helmsman and his mates. The wide range of window apertures would normally be open but any sensible seaman would have shutters ready to close them off, at least to some extent, should he need additional protection from the elements. The second reason was, of course, to remove the gear for handling the mizzen clear above the helmsman. The forecastle did much the same job in removing the gear for handling the two forward spars clear above that for handling the anchors. These two features grew and grew in later ships for everyone apparently relished the ability to stand higher and higher. Amongst friends it was social standing and at war it offered gravity aid to the discharge of missiles.

A suitable ship could now be seen in the mind's eye and we could set out to design it with some confidence in it being at least of the type that Cabot might

have used. Bristol produced a team of Bristol shipwrights under the command
of Mike Blackwell and we all set off on our historical adventure. The Duke of
Edinburgh arrived in horse drawn carriage to set the keel to its work and took
a very close technical interest in what we were up to.

The ship was launched from her building site at Redcliffe Quay in a manner
which typified all that was to follow. As she was lifted by crane into the river the
dull skies opened to sunbeams, a salvo of guns was fired, a multitude of Bristol
people cheered, choirs sang and she floated to her marks. Her builder Mike
Blackwell slipped onboard at once with the lump of beeswax in his hand, to re-
emerge with a broad smile, and the beeswax, to say that she was tight as a drum.
Shipbuilders from time immemorial have taken beeswax onboard just in case
some little leaks might be seen to spoil the day while the wood takes up. It was,
in itself, as historical a scene as anything else that day.

From there everything else followed apace; she was fitted out and rigged,
Captain and crew were appointed and she put to sea for early trials. All punctu-
ated at appropriate intervals with the most moving ceremonies and splendid
parties. In due course it was down to business and Captain David Alan-Williams
and his crew set out to discover once again whether the world was round
and the Americas still moored to the westward of Bristol. On the way they

Matthew under construction at Redcliffe Quay, Bristol during 1995. The heavy horizontal transom piece above the stern forms the base of the poop and also carries the braces for the mainsail.
PHOTO: MAX

experienced a considerable gale and at its height the padre, the Reverend Russell Owen, who confessed to be fairly stupefied with the works of the Lord all about the ship at that time, was asked by another crew member if he could say a few words of prayer. He told the congregation at Redcliffe Church months later that, try as he could, he could not produce words appropriate to the occasion. '*Look here padre,*' said his fellow crew, '*what about: For what we are about to receive...?*'

Meanwhile a considerable reception party was assembling in Newfoundland in the confident expectation that this little sailing vessel would arrive at Bona Vista at eleven o'clock in the morning of Tuesday, 24th June 1997. There is no exaggeration in the use of the word *considerable* for the reception was headed by the Queen and the Duke of Edinburgh, the Premier of Newfoundland, bishops, and other worthies who were there in great numbers. It was icy cold and we were all seated on metal chairs, leading to some concern should our ship be a little late.

It was murky and overcast and quite magical when the sails and spars of this mediaeval ship loomed in sight through the mist over the harbour wall. She entered Bona Vista and quietly moored up in front of us, with her crew in full Cabot costumes, exactly to the minute. Her Captain then came ashore and gravely made his way to pay his dutiful respects to his monarch and her entourage. We and Mike Blackwell also had something to celebrate.

The Lines

One of the beauties of arriving at the lines of a mediaeval ship is that they more or less draw themselves. The constraints of the use of wood overlay nearly every aspect and the others refer to rather simple requirements of form for function. For instance, the midships section – the essential basic form for the ship – has to combine a perimeter of minimum length (to reduce skin friction for light airs) with an ability to sit comfortably on the ground (for safety in grounding and for embarking and unloading cargoes without the need for quays). Again, it has to be able to be subdivided by the plank widths available to the builder.

The re-creation of John Cabot's *Matthew* off Lymington, summer 1996, without her bonnets. The mediaeval ship would have had a completely open poop. PHOTO: MAX

The mediaeval builder did not mess around much with shaping his planks and so the plank widths and the degree of bend he could accept more or less defined the rest of the hull, with some purely practical details. One is that the sensible builder did not put a bend into the length of planking close to the rebates that secured the ends of the plank. It is not easy to get the bend and when achieved does little else for the ship than introduce an unnecessary strain on the plank end securings. Another is that a good width of stern is valuable for both hull capacity and for the lead of the braces in a square rigger or the vangs of a lateen-rigged ship. To this end, therefore, the planks are let run high where they can be secured by a heavy cross-beam called the transom timber or transom piece. This use of parallel sided planking tucked around fairly broad shoulders gives rise to the characteristic sudden lift of the sheer at the bow and at the stern if a transom timber is not fitted.

A little more care has to be taken in developing a respectable sailing ship hull form but it is revealing how easily the hull shape can be drafted using the plank runs rather than the modern conventions of interlacing bow and buttock lines, water-lines and diagonals. These have to be developed eventually for computer and calculations but it does seem something of an intrusion into a quite natural process.

Although drawing the lines of the *Mary Rose* had been something of a rev-elation, especially for performance in very light airs, we did not think that this was relevant to our *Matthew*. Our ship, after all, was to be fitted with twin screws and, with a thousand appointments at ports on both sides of the Atlantic, would not be allowed to dawdle. And so her form is really quite straightforward.

We were less certain about her rudder. Illustrations of ships of the period showed them with a slightly curious paddle-shaped rudder. It looked for all the world as if a side rudder had been hinged to the sternpost. We knew also that such rudders would seem to have been given up for ever within a few years. We

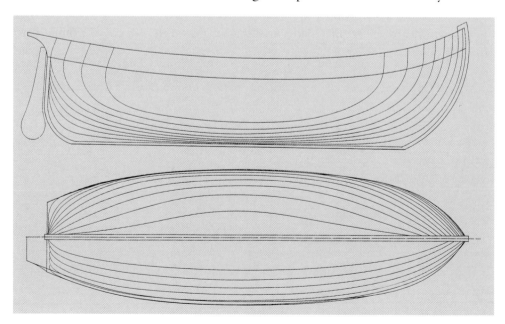

Matthew's lines plan. A mediaeval shape mainly determined by the run of the planking.

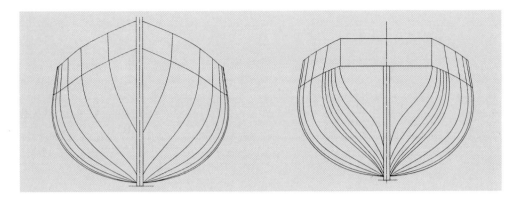

Left: sections from the bow show her barrel-like form which gives her minimum resistance in light winds. Right: sections from the stern with the fine underwater shape to bring water into the rudder.

did not know, on the other hand, if there was any special purpose in the paddle rudder which related to this kind of ship and therefore could not afford to ignore it. The paddle form, like the side rudder, had blade area ahead of its turning axis and so it was essentially a balanced rudder with reduced steering loads. The later close-coupled rudder was more efficient at turning the ship.

We built the apparently correct historical rudder and also a full kit of bits which could be added underwater, if necessary, to convert it into the later form. This was in fact done and found to be a significant improvement.

Performance

From the reports of her voyage across the North Atlantic to Newfoundland she can be seen as making between a quarter and a third wind speed in full sail conditions with everything set and full. Daily she made good something like seventy-five to a hundred miles, although at one point she was doing seven knots, which is a respectable proportion of her theoretical maximum of about ten knots.

To windward she really made nothing as although she could point up to some sixty degrees she would be making twenty degrees of leeway. She is noted as rolling heavily in some conditions – even rolling her bulwarks under in a heavy gale. This was the worst conditions the ship has experienced with wind gusts up to sixty knots and waves noted at forty feet. Her Captain logged laconically that *'ship and crew did well'*.

One or two comments may be appropriate. The original mediaeval ship would very likely have been deeper in the water and sailed more upright to the benefit of its windward performance. Modern safety regulations which required a much greater degree of spare upper hull buoyancy to achieve the required amount of self-righting stability meant that we could not emulate such mediaeval flotation. We had reduced the sail area considerably from that of a mediaeval standard which had the inevitable effect of reducing the all-important hull speed for windward efficiency. It is just possible also that the crews of the mediaeval type of sailing may have been able to kite their sails higher. This would have reduced the angle of heel which is so destructive to windward ability in short fat hulls.

OPPOSITE: The re-creation of John Cabot's *Matthew*, with all five sails set, off St. Michael's mount, Cornwall.
PHOTO: MAX

The small topsail, thought by some to be more for appearance than propulsion, was probably traditionally set for the sole function of being a steadying sail. It is set in the optimum position for such a purpose. I am not sure that such a function was fully appreciated by a modern crew.

Sail Plan

The main novelty to a modern seaman is that the standing rigging was not regarded, as in a modern vessel, as a rigid support system for the mast and to be tended as such. Mediaeval seamen felt free to use it as part of the adjustment system for the set of the sails. Lee rigging was, for instance, slacked away to get the yards around further. When taken aback in such a situation the masts bent a bit until they either did or did not recover support. The rigging was there to aid the masts, not as an essential part of their staying standing. Similarly, the

Colour visual of *Matthew* by Arthur Saluz.

A. SALUZ

parrel system which held the yards to the masts could be eased off to allow the yards to fly or to make it easier to lower them, unlike the modern fixed truss. Another revealing difference lies in the absence of ratlines on the shrouds to help the seamen get aloft and the absence of footropes along the yards for them to work on. The main seamanship was therefore done on deck which meant lowering and raising the heavy yards to make up the sails. Space on deck to handle such a yard that is twice the width of the ship was not easy for our *Matthew* crew. It is in fact not clear how the mediaeval crews handled their yards, which were even longer.

The rig is a clear development of the single square sail vessels of the previous centuries and reflects a purely practical approach to seafaring. For instance, a bigger and heavier ship requires more driving sail area but mast heights were limited to forest trees and it was clearly impractical to handle even wider yards. The next item is that for hulls with the fuller figure, as used for commerce, the centre of hull pressures ranged from amidships to close up to the bow. The mariner had to balance this with his sails and one can appreciate the need to step a second mast well forward and even to project a spar forward of the bow to carry this balancing area. The sail plan of *Matthew* was now closely defined except for the mizzen for which a whole handling deck had to be built. The lateen does not contribute a great deal to the propulsion but makes a sort of aerial rudder for additional balance. It is especially valuable in helping the ship in manoeuvre and remains effective in the wind when the ship's rudder may be ineffective because the ship has stopped.

The only question remaining is why they chose square rig. Practitioners in this rig would wonder if they did anything different. It is the best way to get the biggest sails to drive her. Handling loads are balanced across the mast. Square sails can be backed or filled extremely quickly to stop or even drive the ship astern and also they do not heel the ship to the same degree as other sails even when going to windward.

Construction

Shipbuilding of the period was constrained by several factors. First was the tree available for the keel. Until two logs could be securely fastened end-to-end with sufficient strength to form the backbone of the ship, the size of tree available governed the size of the ship. It was so important as to form the basis of the building contract and was often noted with the other dimensions of the ship. Another was that iron bolt fastenings had traditionally been made by the boatbuilders' blacksmith by hammering a lump into bolt shape. This usually resulted in a fibrous sort of consistency prone to rust rotting up its core. Short iron fastenings such as were used for riveting clincher planking were fine. Shipyard-made long bolt fastenings, however, were regarded as thoroughly unreliable for the securing of important structure or thick planking skins.

To maximise the volume of hull that could be built on a fixed length of keel the shipwrights traditionally added great curved timbers to extend each end and capped them with near vertical stem and sternposts. To build a stout ship without benefit of metal fastenings the construction took the form of a thoroughly interlinked assembly with each component locking to another. The stresses were all taken with a wood-to-wood joint in such a manner that a simple wood peg in shear could lock them. It was not for several years that the metal fastenings improved sufficiently to be trusted to take tension loadings. An apparently small advance that changed the shape of ships for ever.

At the time of *Matthew* we could assume that the construction would have to be one where tension fastenings were absent and the main shear loads taken by wood joints. We could draw some conclusions. The aft plank ends would have to be tucked into a retaining rebate just like the forward ends and therefore *Matthew* would have been a double-ender. The heavy fore and aft and vertical wales which were to be seen on every illustration of ships of the period fell directly into the philosophy of the interlocking and self supporting style of construction. For instance, the fore and aft wales which look like extra thick planks would have been heavy timbers slotted into the main framing. The planking could then be shuttered in between them and the necessary caulking would only load the wale to frame joints. The heavy vertical wales, sometimes thought to be a form of fendering, were slotted for, and clamped over, the longitudinal wales where the hull was likely to be the most stressed. It was all very clever but there is more to it than that. The fore and aft wales were spaced accurately to accommodate standard plank widths. The builders did not need to shape their planking and the seamen need carry only the simplest of replacement spares.

We built her in the historical manner as best we could and, belt and braces being our watchword, we used aluminium bronze bolts throughout in place of the wooden pegs and unreliable iron. All seemed to go quite easily with the exception of getting the planking around the robust curves of her stern.

The hearty Bristol shipwrights were very polite and only swore about their problems in my absence. It was a simple problem in its way. The planks were steamed before being wrapped around the hull and as they cooled the moisture evaporated from the timber and they would split. Lesser shipwrights might have taken to the bottle or at least to laminating but our chaps were of greater stuff and eventually managed to get the stern planked up. The problem was that modern shipwrights use steam bending to shape wood in place of the oil bending which would have been used. In oil bending the timber is copiously anointed with a suitable light oil as it lies on an oak chip fire. The timber is turned and coated until the oil is not only well into the timber but has heated it as hot as steam. The difference is that as the timber cools to its new shape, the oil does not evaporate and the timber does not split. I saw oil bending still being used in an Indian shipyard, but unfortunately only after the stern of *Matthew* had been planked up.

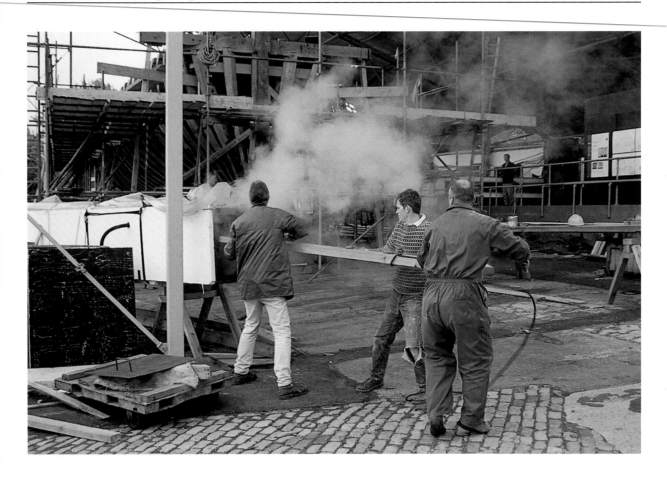

Matthew – loading the steam pot which softens the timber for bending round the hull. PHOTO: MAX

Authenticity

Authenticity means different things to different people. Some prefer the actual article as used by some famous historical person. Others would rather see it reconstructed as it would have been in all its working glory. The former tendency seem to prefer items, which are old and may be dull, for their personal closeness to the famous while the rest are possibly more interested in how it all worked. Even then authenticity can be no more than an attempt as, very often, the actual craft skills have changed and the actual materials have been 'improved'. Again there are modern safety regulations which cannot be ignored.

So we inquired carefully of our clients, as we always do, as to which elements of authenticity they required. We said we thought that we could deliver almost complete authenticity to the point where she could be used for research into the seafaring characteristics. The main exceptions to full authenticity would be in the difficulties in the acquisition of completely comparable timber and the need to meet certain statutory requirements. In addition, for her main voyaging, she would have to be fitted with power propulsion, full accommodation for a modern crew and all the modern navigation and communication equipment. We would not expect the shipbuilders to build with the tools of the period and we

would use modern fastenings to hold her together for a longer life, but she would otherwise be built in the manner of the period of the original.

We proposed, and it was accepted, that all the twentieth century aspects of the ship should be removable to leave her in fifteenth century condition for serious assessment.

We made an unscheduled visit to the site just after Christmas when she was building to find that the whole of the poop deck had been raised eight inches without reference and this was the end of any real effort towards authenticity. By the time she set off she had been fitted with a completely non-authentic whipstaff steering, the ballast had been taken from inside the ship and added to the keel and the engine had been moved from more or less amidships (where the ship's hold would have carried the main loads) to right forward and a power windlass added to handle the mooring anchors. We were sympathetic to the reasons for these changes. The poop was lifted to accommodate the height of modern men and the ballast and machinery changes certainly improved the crew accommodation and the steering was more direct than sailing by helm orders. Our sadness really lay in the dashing of our hopes to find out more about mediaeval sailing.

Matthew under construction in 1996 at Redcliffe Quay, Bristol (thought to be the place where John Cabot embarked for his 1497 voyage).
Photo: Max

Aileach

Design for a West Highland birlinn

16th Century *&* 1991/92

Dimensions			
Length overall		39.67 feet	12.20 metres
Waterline length		35.50 feet	10.80 metres
Beam		10.83 feet	3.05 metres
Draft		2.00 feet	0.60 metres
Sail area		360 square feet	33.50 square metres
Construction	Wood		
Rowing crew	16 places		

The Project

Fairly early in 1990 we were approached by Wallace Clark about designing a reconstruction of a West Highland birlinn. Not just any old birlinn that is, but one that might be thought to be a reconstruction of one of the Lord of the Isles' own private craft. Not any old birlinn from their four hundred year history either but one from the middle of the sixteenth century when they reached their peak of development. Furthermore it might not really be a birlinn at all but more of a nyvaig.

What is more Wallace wished first to voyage from the West of Ireland to Scotland to demonstrate the ancient West Coast links. Then it was to be proof of birlinn seaworthiness and all round ability in taking what would be a forty foot open boat on a voyage to the Faeroes and, of course, back. We knew of his voyaging in his yacht *Wild Goose* and that he had crewed a thirty foot curragh from Derry to Iona and had done his time on Tim Severin's curragh *Brendan* before the transatlantic voyage. We knew also that he was working in partnership with his son Miles and also Ranald MacDonald, the twenty-fourth hereditary Captain of Clanranald, and his son Andrew, all accomplished seamen; it was a formidable and serious assembly of the maritime talent which would be required for operating such a vessel.

Birlinns and their variations were the galleys of the Western Isles of Scotland and nearby Ireland, developed to suit local materials and conditions from a Viking ancestry. Somerled, the original Lord of the Isles, ruler of some five

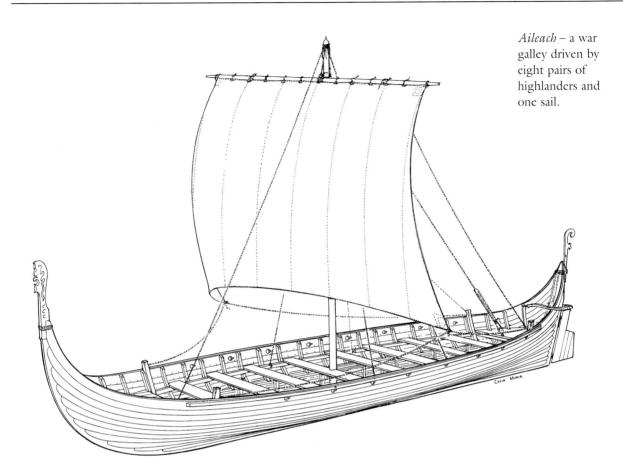

hundred islands in the twelfth century, was apparently the mainspring for their development. Wallace calculated that it was likely that there would be two or three hundred such galleys at any one time and that there must have been, in their history, some four thousand built.

The real end of their history was Hanoverian resolve to 'extirpate the vipers'. The Scottish galleys were no match for the three-masted English warships and their big guns, and that was the end of them. Wallace also notes that it was not a Scottish habit to use their galleys for burial or any other use of sentiment which might yield definitive remains for study. Possibly due to the climate, old galleys did better service as fuel for the winter fires. There are, therefore, no positive artefacts yet found although there was a useful supply of tomb carved depictions, but there was Mike Jarvis, Professor of Agricultural Chemistry at Glasgow University, whose passion is Scottish galleys. He had researched all there was to know with academic thoroughness. Mike Jarvis guided us through the evidence and we quickly agreed that a galley shown on a tomb of 1528 in Rodel, Harris, illustrated a fully practical vessel in excellent detail. What is more, there was little that conflicted with the other carvings and graffiti and we thought that we could go forward on these lines.

Our job therefore was to consider how the Viking ship might have developed for the particular raiding and trading uses in the Isles and also what elements of change would have been likely to optimise the construction with the different timbers available. Two matters stood out from Rodel and the others. They showed a vessel with a stern centreline rudder in place of the side rudders of earlier vessels. Secondly, the manner in which the plank ends were secured was different to the Scandinavian pattern.

A centreline rudder is possibly more effective and certainly less trouble for the crew than side rudders and was a logical development, especially for the smaller galleys such as our birlinn. The other matter, the plank end housings – the 'hood (or wood) ends' of shipwrightery – were more interesting. Instead of being secured into relatively small rebates in the stem and sternposts, as did the Vikings and as wooden boatbuilders do today, they were lapped into quite large stem and stern members with the plank lines carved on to simulate the Scandinavian. The Scottish construction is essentially stronger and more suited to well sprung clincher planking. Presumably this practical improvement was possible using local grown timber – probably sessile oak which one would expect to be the oak of the Highlands' Western Isles.

The value of strong end securings for the upper planks coupled with a minimum of support in the centrebody allows the craft to flex suitably in a seaway without involving stress points. Apart from the simple matter of hull strength such stress points affect the natural rhythm of the flexing, especially important for a high quality rowing vessel.

The Faeroes Voyage

The main voyage started from Castle Tiorram near Moidart, the ruins of a MacDonald fortress on the Moidart peninsula, outward bound for Thorshaven some three hundred and sixty miles away. Andrew McDonald and his crew slipped up through the Sound of Sleat and the Kyles and then across the North Minch to have their radio fixed at Stornoway. A broken rudder required an RNLI side trip to Stornoway and a couple of weeks of the seaman's three R's – Rest, Repairs and Rotten weather. Four days later they were surfing along at twelve knots again and made the Isle of Suduroy, the most southerly of the Faeroes, and on to Thorshaven next day. Two days later with the legendary Trondur Pattursson embarked and 're-victualled with whale meat' they averaged 2.8 knots for a two hundred and seventy-five mile passage back to Loch Gareloch.

This was perhaps the headline voyage for the project but *Aileach* has also boated extensively about the coasts of Ireland and Scotland. In a purely historical spirit they seemed to have accepted the Highland hospitality of several distinguished distilleries. In the same tireless quest after authenticity they are known to have left a note 'gone to rape and pillage' on their ship when they went ashore.

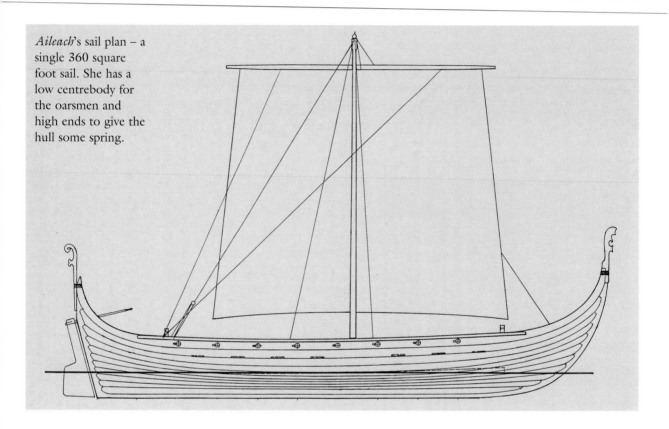

Aileach's sail plan – a single 360 square foot sail. She has a low centrebody for the oarsmen and high ends to give the hull some spring.

Hull flexing is of course a feature of the Viking type to the point where the longer ships were labelled as *snekirs*, or snakes. As these were often the private vessels of the chiefs, in fact the yachts of their day, it is a pleasant thought to consider how our yacht clubs would now be titled if they had followed Norse nomenclature rather than the Dutch *jacht* for their pleasure craft.

Our birlinn (*nyvaig* is just Gaelic for a small ship) was required to have eight pairs of oars and some forty feet in length. Her shape is really ruled by the classic Viking ship form and based around the eight rooms a side for each rower. We planned her construction to give her the well-sprung hull. If we veered in any direction it lay in giving her probably heavier scantlings than a fully experienced galley builder would have given the personal vessel of the Lord of the Isles. However, we felt that something in reserve in this area might help us sleep better when the ship was at sea.

Also, to help everyone sleep when she was away, we all agreed on fitting her with a fair amount of foam plastics buoyancy. A wooden vessel without ballast is not supposed to sink anyway but the problems lie in bailing her out should she be swamped. Unless there is ample freeboard the sea is likely to sweep back on board with the slightest change in trim, which is especially fragile in a swamped vessel.

Aileach was in any case either ballasted or deep with stores for her voyaging. Wallace Clark had her filled up to test the practicality of her flooded flotation with this added buoyancy before he took her to sea.

Aileach was built by the MacDonalds of Moville, a family of boatbuilders who are by repute descended from some MacDonalds who made a somewhat swift tactical move to Ireland after the '45. The historical connections were a bonus. However, when I went to visit them I saw some beautifully planked clincher boats of their own design and build. Getting clincher planking to look right is far from easy, in fact a great skill which somehow contributes to performance as well as to appearance. Any Lord of the Isles would, as can be seen by the photographs, have appreciated their work.

I am aware of only two things of importance that broke during her quite testing voyaging. Early on, a rather poor mast which might have survived tightly strapped up in the modern manner could not cope with the flexing natural to her rig. Interestingly enough it was replaced with one of better timber and smaller dimensions which has lasted ever since. The other was much more important. The rudder stock broke in strong conditions some thirty miles north of Cape Wrath and after a tiring time trying repairs and substitutes Andrew McDonald decided to call for help and she was plucked in by the Stromness Arun class lifeboat.

It is easy sitting warm and dry ashore to point out that the rudder had been built with cross grained stock but it is also a lesson for us to learn that we might have made sure that she had a proper and effective second steering system for offshore voyaging. We have a sneaky feeling that the Vikings, with their twin side rudders, may have had the better ocean faring alternative.

The Lines

As a 'motor sailer' there is no need to optimise sailing performance in light airs by looking, for instance, for minimum skin area and laminar flow. More important is the need to optimise the work for the rowers. This means that the entry and indeed the water exit aft should be fine to iron out the variations of speed and resistance as the rowers heave at their oars. As important perhaps is that a fine bow will reduce the bow wave which can affect the efficiency of the forward pair of oars. It is possible that the fine stern has the same effect for the stroke oarsmen but it is more likely that it is just a method of getting the passing water smoothly and efficiently away from the comparatively full body required to carry the weight of her crew. This full body is essentially forward of amidships both to gain some value for getting her to windward and to take the push from the oars.

Overall, however, the shape is dominated by the need to get her planked and for the planking there are three criteria. First, of course, is that they must be able to be cut from the trees available to the builder. Second is that they must not be

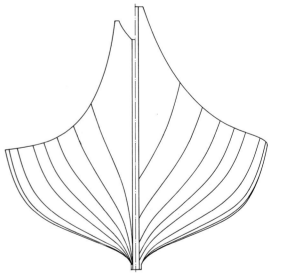

Aileach's body plans, from the bow (right) and stern (left) are almost identical. The fine underwater hull flares out to accommodate the rowing crew.

83

too wide in themselves in any case so that the normal drying out does not cause them to split. Third is that they must wrap around the hull and, in addition to what you might call the flat bending of the plank, they must also have just the correct amount of edge bend to give the hull the necessary additional springiness. Many modern builders in wood will steam or laminate it so that the planks will lie easily around the hull curves, not realising that in doing so they are, in part, interfering with and in fact probably reducing the performance of the boat at sea.

Walk Through

Open boats do not present much of a walk through – just eight thwarts and short raised platforms at each end. The crew added a centreline walking plank which we might have planned into her except our feeling that every pound of weight would add load to a muscle-powered vessel. They also added a seat for the helmsman – a feature with which we are personally sympathetic. For their offshore voyaging they were able to remove some thwarts which were lashed into place and erect some humble cabin structures. They noted that the rowing rooms were a bit on the small side for the dimensions of modern crew. This may be due to thigh rowing instead of the traditional shoulder rowing, but I think that another time I would specify shorter oars, probably fourteen foot in place of sixteen, and propose a little more length of ship.

Aileach: sleeping arrangement for fifteen crew, at anchor or in harbour.

We were concerned about the geography of a rowing crew when night fell on mooring and we made the sketch, shown here, which I think tells enough about the necessary bonding of the crews of Highland galleys and the attractiveness of beaching the boat every night.

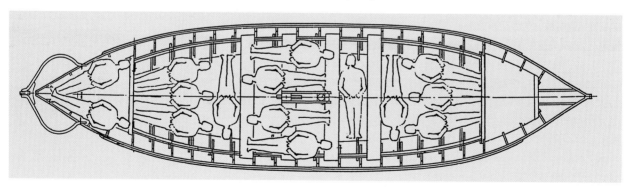

Galley Racing

We hoped that *Aileach* would stimulate an interest in the galley and this would seem to be reflected in several new books and a greatly increased public interest in the subject. We had hoped that it would develop into international racing, initially between Scotland and Ireland. We developed draft rules where any number

of crew could embark as long as the same crew was disembarked at the end of the race. They could sail, row, paddle, swim or take any action they liked to get to the finishing line and in one version the galley could be any size they liked. The sting in the tail was that the course would include a portage where the crew had to carry their craft across a neck of land. At no time could any of the athletes onboard be at rest and it would be a full contest of nautical mind and muscle.

Such a race would involve all the Corinthian elements for maritime sport and would allow the development of craft and contestants on purely natural criteria. It did not go unnoticed that the TV might relish the vision of craft roaring in to land to be picked up by the housed oars and rushed across to be relaunched and wing their way onwards.

At the time there was a great deal of enthusiasm and talk but I suppose it is a bit risky to set out as a sponsor to develop what might, despite some three thousand years of galley history, be considered as a new sport.

Aileach makes landfall south-east of Islay, 1991.
PHOTO: MILES CLARK

Mary Rose

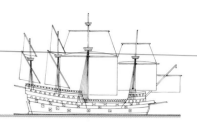

A new look at Henry VIII's flagship

16th Century

Dimensions		
Hull length	136.50 feet	41.60 metres
Hull beam	38.30 feet	11.70 metres
Construction	Wood	
Crew	Approximately 700 at capsize	
Armament	Approximately 70 cannon	

History of *Mary Rose*

The *Mary Rose* was built to the order of King Henry VIII and her keel was laid in Portsmouth Dockyards in 1509. Built as a 'King's Ship', her original role was partly as a Royal transport of some 600 tons capacity and partly as a warship. In 1536 she was rebuilt for the sole role of warship and heavily loaded with armament, and was probably one of the first to use a broadside through hull ports. In this mode she was armed with fifteen bronze cannons, fifty-six iron cannons, some seventy hand guns, and two hundred and fifty longbows. She was rated as one of the world's most powerful battleships until 1545, when she capsized.

Naval architects are constitutionally averse to having their mistakes drawn back to the surface of the sea and put on exhibition as examples of their work. *Mary Rose*, however, was by reputation the finest example of the sailing ship of her period before some quite elementary mistakes would seem to have been made in her last refit. Naval architects would seem to make the same mistakes every few hundred years and it seems likely that *Mary Rose, HMS Captain* in 1870, and possibly some other ships, all fell victim to what seems a fairly obvious approach to design. If you want to put heavy weights onboard, put them on a low and watertight deck. The analogy is the raft – marvellous as long as it sits flat in the water but liable to capsize extremely quickly if it develops enough angle of heel to get water on deck. *Mary Rose* was apparently re-gunned on her last refit and the guns were enormous with barrels twelve feet long and bigger than the guns of, for instance, *HMS Victory*. They were fitted to the lower deck which when the gun ports were opened became no more and no less than a raft.

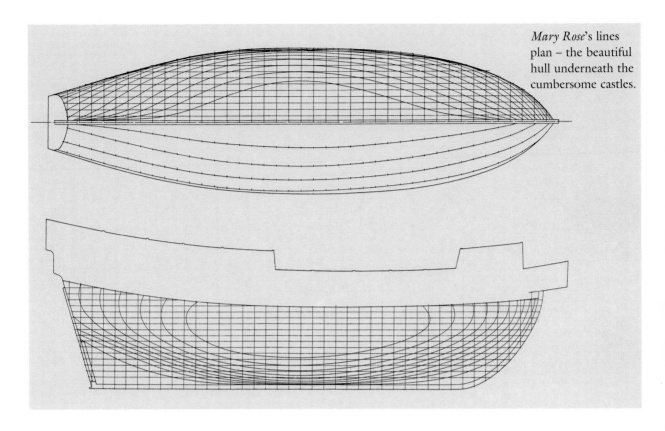

Mary Rose's lines plan – the beautiful hull underneath the cumbersome castles.

When the fighting men went to one side of the ship to shout defiance at the 'frogs' the ship would probably heel to an amount which she probably experienced under sail in normal duty. Water flooding in through the gun ports onto the lower deck, however, would remove the greater part of the buoyancy of the upper hull. The lower deck would act like a rather poor raft trying to support the whole ship, which would capsize and sink in what must have felt like an instant.

It is difficult to put the dreadful tragedy of her sinking out of mind even after all these years but her recovery has allowed us to appreciate that she was of a very high standard of hull design indeed. I was lucky enough to be asked by the archaeological team to translate the dimensioned sections as they were taken off the hull, both below water and later above, into a lines plan. We were astonished at the sophistication of the form which appeared on the drawing board. It was quite shamefully clever compared with what we had been producing and we thought that we were right up in modern practice. The actual beauty of the lines speak out for themselves and they are so much easier to appreciate when divorced from the sodden dark wood to be seen in the ship hall.

There are many aspects and I would not put them in particular order. However, the main eye opener is that the shape of the hull is such as to positively enhance the possibility of the establishment of laminar flow to be produced around the hull at low water speeds. Laminar, or smooth, flow markedly reduces the skin friction and thereby importantly reduces the drag of

Mary Rose – sections from the bow (left) – with her full above water hull combined with a fine underwater shape.

Sections from the stern (right) – one of the earliest instances of a transom construction.

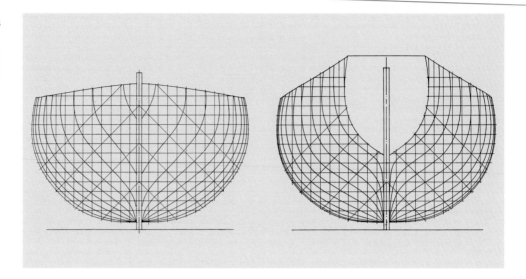

the hull. A sailing ship, without any power except the winds of heaven, is at its most vulnerable when those winds are light. Picture, for instance, *Mary Rose* trying to navigate amongst sands and rocks in spring tides and light winds. Furthermore, when the waterflow over your hull is the only source of any windward ability, hull speed in light airs is critical. Next look at the careful balance between a windward working hull form and the minimum of skin area to drag through the sea. Look again at the beautiful balance between bow and stern and the way a quite full upper bow profile (valuable to keep the bow buoyant and to help reduce synchronous pitching) fairs sweetly into a fine entry. Note also that this fine entry encompasses plenty of bow steering surface. The function of the rudder is to set the ship slightly askew and let these bow surfaces turn the ship. *Mary Rose* ought to have been excellent in steering and in manoeuvring.

Two other items may be of interest. Note that at the bow the last six feet or so of planking has very little bend in it. The builders could secure the ends of these planks in the stem rebate and fasten them securely to several frames before applying the loads necessary to bend them to the hull form. Next look at the stern where the hull body planking is fastened to a flat transom. This is a quite early use of such a construction and implies the employment of good strong fastenings to hold them to the transom fashion pieces or framings. Good iron fastenings were expensive and this illustrates that she was built to the highest standards with expense, as would be proper for a King's ship, a secondary consideration.

There is one other feature of the ship which took our fancy. In illustrations of the period the builders would seem to have used highly decorated short planks fitted vertically to fill in the topsides between the bulwark rail and the topgallant bulwark rail – two levels of the shipside above the main deck. These turn out to be a blindage of portable arrow slots. The bowman lifted out the short plank in front of him, discharged his arrow and whipped the plank back in place as fast as he could before any enemy arrow could be fired back.

Incidentally this more or less horizontal arrow firing illustrates that a great deal of marine fighting at that time must have been done at close quarters. The blindage would seem to inhibit firing high to rain arrows down onto the enemy decks. Interestingly, the recovered blinds are without trace of decoration which makes one suspect that this royal ship had one set for show and one for warfare.

As part of our interest in the *Mary Rose* I was asked, before her recovery, to produce some kind of drawing of what she might, just might, have been like. This slightly light-hearted drawing is reproduced above.

An early visual of *Mary Rose*, before she was raised. Note the many large guns on the lower deck, and the anti-boarding netting which trapped so many when she capsized. PHOTO: COLIN MUDIE

H.M.S. Victory

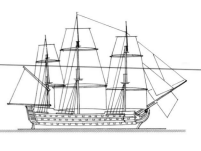

Nelson's great ship

18th Century

Dimensions		
Sparred length	328.00 feet	100.00 metres
Hull length	226.00 feet	69.00 metres
Sparred beam	197.00 feet	60.00 metres
Hull beam	52.00 feet	15.80 metres
Draft	20.00 feet	6.00 metres
Displacement	3,500 tons	
Construction	Wood	
Armament	104 guns	
Crew at Trafalgar	850	

First let me hasten to say that *Victory* is included in these pages out of admiration and the pleasure and education I have had from her. Let me equally quickly add that her keel was laid in Single Dock, Chatham in 1759 and she was built to the designs of Sir Thomas Slade, Senior Surveyor at that time to the Royal Navy. She was one of twelve large ships of the line ordered by George II but naval affairs were going so well in the Seven Years War that she was built in a rather leisurely manner – six years in place of the usual five. The name *Victory* itself celebrates the naval successes of the period and it is said to particularly refer to those in North America. A further reflection of those successes was that she was not actually required when she was completed and was not put in commission for a further thirteen years.

Her statistics are notable. She has a hull length of only sixty-nine metres but her rig extends this by about half as much again (thirty-one metres). Her beam is under sixteen metres but with her stunsails spread she set sails extending to sixty metres.

Her displacement was, and presumably still is, about three thousand five hundred tons but she embarked some five hundred tons of equipment and crew when she went to war. At Trafalgar she carried eight hundred and fifty persons into battle and fought with over one hundred guns. Thirty of those fired cannon balls of over fourteen kilos weight. Now she is no less than two hundred and forty years old and still a pleasure and instruction to thousands of visitors.

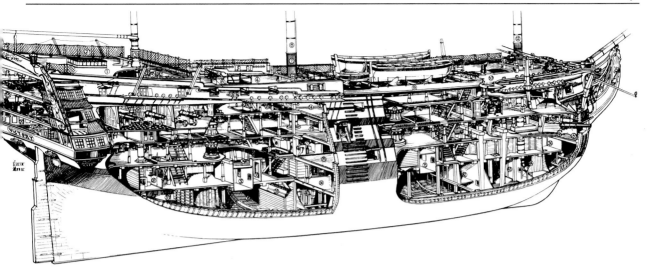

My first real acquaintance with *Victory* came in 1959 when Dudley Pope, the well known naval historian and maritime author, embarked on a book on Trafalgar called *England Expects*. To illustrate the complexity and layout of Nelson's flagship he asked me to make a drawing of her – a drawing of the rather technical cutaway type which goes into detail of construction and layout, etc.

Armed with this objective I was given generous permission by her Captain to explore every detail of the ship without restrictions as to place and time. Some of the ship was under reconstruction and some parts reflected changes of use since she was last in battle in, I think, 1808. As she had been a prime and victorious warship every aspect of her had to have had logic and purpose and I took it all very seriously. For instance, I found a traditional shot garland around the foot of the foremast deep in the ship. The shot, apparently little cannon balls of about a kilo in weight, were still in place and the whole had been enamelled white, which I knew to be a military characteristic. For the life of me I could not fathom their purpose. Why would you have ready-use ammunition for a quite sizeable cannon in the forward bilges where one shot might sink the ship? Was it, I wondered, a symptom of the harsh prison regimes in ancient warships or a reflection of true British pluck that would fight boarders all the way down to the bilges? Next day, a little deeper in the ship, I found an abandoned billiard table, reflecting perhaps the off duty pastime of previous ship keepers. My drawing includes that non-historic shot garland at the foot of the foremast.

Victory reflects a period of total technical ability and competence, designed and built by masters of their trades or professions. Such was their ease with the technology that, like master craftsmen in any discipline, they took time to decorate and set off their work. *Victory* may not be the most decorated of warships over the centuries but has a remarkable blend of gold leaf and authority which easily indicates her as a flagship. She is an illustration of the end product of thousands of years of a particular arm of sailing ship development. Nothing really much better ever occurred for sea warfare until the advent of metal plates and hissing steam brought in new opportunities.

Dunbrody

An Irish barque of the 19th Century

1845 & 2000

Dimensions		
Sparred length	176.00 feet	53.70 metres
Hull length	120.00 feet	36.60 metres
Waterline length	106.00 feet	32.30 metres
Hull beam	28.00 feet	8.50 metres
Draft	11.50 feet	3.50 metres
Sail area	8,465 square feet	786 square metres
Displacement	440 tons	
Construction	Wood	
Crew	18	
Passengers	176	

The Project

The timber supplies of Europe were exhausted after the Napoleonic wars and particularly by the naval aspects of those wars. For instance, the building of one line-of-battle ship required some seventy-five acres (30 hectares) of first-class forest timber of eighty to a hundred years of growth. On that basis, the sixty ships that fought the battle of Trafalgar represented over seven square miles of ancient forests.

To import timber from the forests of North America would require even more ships. The only and rather obvious solution was to build the ships over there to transport the timber across to Europe. Various restrictive shipping acts were repealed and the most amazing bonanza in shipping commenced. Timber ships by the hundreds were built more or less wherever a shipyard could be sited close to trees. The ships embarked timber and sailed for Europe. They paid for themselves in two or three voyages, much like the tanker boom after the last world war. Consequently there were no particular commercial pressures for them to have a long life. They could be built of softwoods with iron fastenings, work for a few years under Lloyd's survey approvals, and then disperse to other service.

Dunbrody was one of these. She was built in Quebec in 1845 by Thomas Hamilton Oliver, a renowned Irish shipbuilder, for William Graves, a timber

merchant of New Ross in County Wexford in the south of Ireland. Thomas Oliver built over a hundred such vessels in his lifetime and such was the production facility at his yard that it is known that the 458 ton *Dunbrody* was built in six winter months. The icing up of the St. Lawrence kept seamen ashore in the winter and added numbers to the construction gangs.

From our point of view, however, she is an example of a pinnacle of sailing ship design. Production methods were honed to a commercial art. Ship speed was, within reason, less valuable than reliability and capacity for their commercial purposes. They might be considered as the last generation to be totally self supporting for every aspect of their seafaring. Shortly afterwards the spread of steam tugs to commercial harbours relieved sailing ships of the need for good slow speed performance and the companion requirement for ultra reliability of manoeuvre in restricted waters and for berthing.

Where our *Dunbrody* becomes important in the scheme of things is that her life coincided with the Irish famine years and the great emigrations of the Irish to the New World. The timber ships, having discharged their timber, looked for some other cargo for their west-bound voyages. The preferred cargoes of pig

An Arthur Saluz visual of the barque *Dunbrody* as she will look.

93

iron or limestone took little space and their empty and spacious holds could be quickly and cheaply fitted out with simple accommodation. They could then embark emigrants urgent and anxious to get away from the quite dreadful conditions of the great famine. Some ships succumbed to greed and packed people into their holds and treated them very badly indeed with many becoming ill and dying *en route*. *Dunbrody* is thought to have been one of the better ships in this trade but even so a quick assessment of her passenger numbers comes to a conclusion of the order of a hundred and seventy-six persons. This in a vessel only some thirty odd metres on deck.

Incidentally, her passenger accessible lavatories were probably limited to two on deck forward and probably four below; a ratio of close to one for every thirty persons compared with the one for six or eight we work to these days. Fares at about £3 a head brought *Dunbrody* a revenue of an additional £500 for comparatively little expense, as the emigrant passengers often had to provide their own food. The voyage to Canada would take somewhere between three and eight weeks depending on conditions.

The accommodation was a range of carpenter-built two-tier berths each some six foot square and allocated to four persons (usually of the same family). Young males were berthed forward, married couples amidships, and the young girls lived at the aft end of this accommodation. The ship's own crew lived in their normal accommodation with the hands in the forecastle right forward and the officers in some comfort right aft. Because these ships were not specially built for the passenger trade they were largely without deckhouses or deckworks where the emigrants might shelter in the less clement conditions and commonly they were restricted to the hold. The only deckhouse was often no more than a tiny caboose for the cook, hot coals below decks being taboo with a timber cargo. Even this modest compartment facility was inaccessible in bad weather and there are accounts of it being swept clean off the decks of some ships in severe conditions.

The icing of the St. Lawrence confined the emigrant-out and timber-home voyages to between April and September and limited them to two round trips each year. For the winter months the ships worked cargoes to southern Europe and the West Indies. *Dunbrody* is recorded as carrying guano from Peru, which meant around the Horn.

Our *Dunbrody* was the brainchild of marine artist Garrett Fallon who convinced the John F. Kennedy Trust of New Ross that they should build and exhibit such a ship. It would be a remembrance of the famine period and a tribute to the emigration of the Kennedy family from their Irish homestead near New Ross.

When asked by the Project Manager Sean Reidy to design the reconstruction, we rather assumed that the vessel would be well documented, that there might be photographs and almost certainly a half model. In the end we were reduced to the entries in Lloyd's Register and a copy of an initial certificate to allow her to proceed from Quebec to New Ross for registration. However, from Lloyd's

we knew that she was of 109.8 feet in registered length, beam of 26.7 feet, had a depth in hold of 18.7 feet, and a registered tonnage of 458. Further it told us that she was a three-masted barque. From her initial certificate we read that she had a standing bowsprit, was square sterned, carvel built with 'no galleries' and had a man figurehead. From a later survey report (1855) we had the sizes of her ground tackle, her boats and the fact that she was zinc sheathed in 1854. A valuable additional note says that she had a proper passenger deck, which was not always the case. Other research indicated that the words 'flush decked' could be taken to mean that she did not have any poop structure but that she might have a topgallant forecastle deck. This short raised deck at the bow was in any case necessary for the additional space required for handling both the anchors and the running rigging coming in from the bowsprit.

With this as our starting point we set to work to meet these criteria and as ever found that they more or less defined an eminently practicable vessel. We still, however, live in some dread that a half model, rumoured to be in some Irish attic, might be discovered and that it might be so different that we will all have to start again.

The re-creation of the 1847 wooden barque *Dunbrody* which took up to 176 Irish emigrants on each voyage to North America and returned with cargoes of timber. Her hull length is 120 feet and her total length is 176 feet.

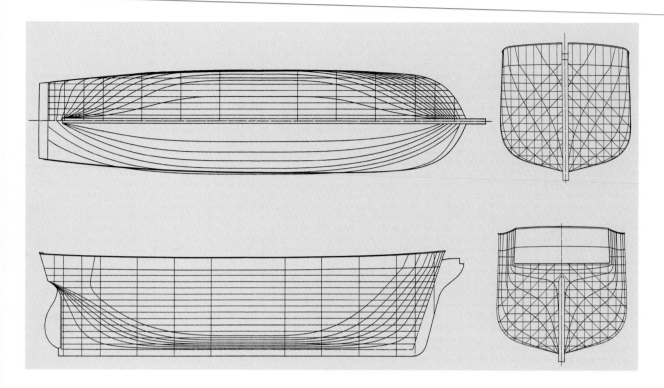

Dunbrody's lines plan illustrates the full bodied capacity required for a cargo vessel.

The original *Dunbrody* stayed in the Graves family ownership for some twenty-four years. She was then sold to Cardiff and later registered in Bremen in 1874. The following year she was stranded and lost near Belle Isle off the coast of Labrador. A hard working and wide ranging life of thirty years must be a tribute to her builders and her owners and makes her a very good example for our reconstruction.

The Lines

There is not a great deal to say about the lines of *Dunbrody*. They are typical of the commercial sailing ship of Victorian times, heavily circumscribed by the need to combine maximum capacity within the tonnage measurement regulations which formed the basis of harbour dues and other costs. That said, I think we can admire the manner in which these purely commercial factors are combined in a sweet form with the depth and hydrofoil form for an efficient windward performance. The steeply rising buttocks aft indicate a hull which, if overdriven, would suck down and induce pooping but whoever heard of a timber drogher being raced in strong winds and high seas? The bow is efficient for windward work and fills out to an almost semicircular deck. This considerable forward buoyancy will keep the bow high at sea and should help to keep her decks free.

One can also appreciate the easily planked form with considerable lengths of the hull which take more or less straight planks. The tiny size of the rudder is

something of amazement to the modern yacht designer but look at the quite long and easy form leading to it and the effective underwater bow which actually turns the ship. The uncompromising flat rectangular shape of the transom is not to everyone's taste and there are those who would round it off a bit, especially the lower outboard corners. As the original shipbuilders could have done this rather more easily than plank up to the sharp corner I suspect that it has some value. My own view is that the sharp corner produces tip vortices which reduce the drag and suck-in of water to the transom in the vulnerable conditions when this is immersed by the sea in strong weather. But all in all the lines are considerably more shapely than might be expected for a purely commercial craft built on what looks like a bit of a production line.

Dunbrody in her drydock at New Ross, Ireland, 1999.
PHOTO: ROSEMARY MUDIE

Walk Through

The original *Dunbrody* was blessed by a permanent lower deck for the full length of the vessel. Many of her contemporaries did not have this and for the passenger service to Canada a temporary deck had to be constructed, as well as the fairly rudimentary accommodation required. This deck was noted by Lloyd's with apparent satisfaction as being more than one and a half inches thick and

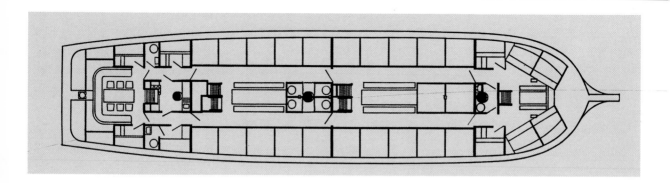

The general layout of *Dunbrody*. The twenty-two rectangles in the centre body represent two-tier berths, each for four persons.

being properly supported by beams. It was not altogether common in the timber ships as such a deck interfered with the loading of the timber which was made through shipside hatches in the bow and stern. It is likely, therefore, that *Dunbrody* may have been intended by the Graves family from the very beginning for the emigrant trade. They would, after all, have seen the need for it all around them in County Wexford. A slightly suspicious confirmation of this possible intention is that the dimensions of the ship lend themselves to a range of six foot berths from one end of the ship to the other.

The officers lived aft, as was the tradition. She would have had a saloon furnished in dark polished timber – possibly native American walnut – with polished brass fittings. The large dining table would have had a swinging rack over for bottles and condiments and the settee would have been upholstered. The Captain and his officers would have had individual cabins and a WC compartment with a lead lavatory pan so well finished that you could mistake it for porcelain. Chart work, log writing and such matters as the ship's accounts were all carried out at the saloon table. There would also have been a pantry for the preparation of the officers' victuals which would have been stored in the space under the accommodation. Access to the deck was by a companion stair into a deck hatch incorporated in a skylight structure. Our *Dunbrody*'s aft accommodation follows this pattern but, for modern times, has to include a chart room with the usual electronic clutter and, with the main engine room under the accommodation, has to make provision for vents and exhausts. The ship's galley has also had to come aft and modern regulators require it to be lined in fireproof steel.

Our *Dunbrody* has a watertight bulkhead division between the officers' quarters and the emigrant decks. These are built as reconstructions with carpenter sawn rough timber two-tier berths lining the shipside. On the centreline are equally rough tables and stools and at the foot of the mainmast, four partitioned-off bucket lavatories. There are three companions or ladders to deck hatches and these are the sole sources of ventilation and light. There are no portholes or decklights and oil lights had to burn continuously to give light for the passengers. Their food had, at least nominally, to be cooked in the deck galley and this was really only practical in good conditions. One suspects that a fair degree of freelance cooking went on below decks to add to the stuffy ambience that must have existed when the hatches were closed in bad weather.

Dunbrody – a cargo-carrying barque typical of the period before steam.

Forward of the passenger space was the forecastle where the professional seamen lived and it was not a lot better. Being in the eyes of the ship with the maximum hull motion it may even have been a great deal worse. There were open bunks for twelve and a table and stools. Access was from a deck companion; food cooked in the galley on deck had to be brought below. Again there was very little natural light and the washroom accommodation was in two tiny shipside compartments at the break of the forecastle.

Access between the compartments would have been by wooden doors in simple wooden bulkheads. Our *Dunbrody* has to be fitted with watertight bulkheads fitted with steel 'six dog' watertight doors and have an additional bulkhead amidships. We have no objection to the safety such equipment adds but it is sometimes difficult to pretend that it was natural kit in the 1840s.

Sail Plan

At a glance the rig of *Dunbrody* is not unfamiliar – similar in fact to that to be seen in other ships at any gathering of tall ships these days. Her rig, however, is of a quite different era and designed and built for operation in a quite different maritime scene. Notice first how much sail this humble timber ship can set, for she was not a clipper racing to get the first cargo home. Notice the bowsprit sticking out half the length of her hull and the sheer loftiness of the rig.

Essentially such a ship, very vulnerable in light airs, needed to catch every zephyr she could to develop the all important hull speed which would give her a chance to windward in light airs.

Another point to notice is that her basic sailing fit-out – the lower masts and the standing bowsprit – are not only very strong but also heavily supported with standing rigging. While these are heavier than you will see in the ships of today, the upper masts and the jibboom get progressively lighter as they extend from these stout spars until they become mere walking sticks supported by gossamer threads. The result is that the upper and outer part of the rig flexes in what would now be thought to be a quite alarming manner. There are several interesting logics involved. First, that as the greatest extent of canvas is only set in light airs there is no need to mount it on great heavy spars. Second, that flexing is a 'good thing'. Flexing absorbs wind gusts with minimum strains to ship or rig and returns some of the driving energy when the gusts ease. Third, comes the aspect of safety. Should the ship be struck with a sudden microburst of high speed wind the lighter spars act as a safety fuse and break before the ship is knocked flat. This safety function was often aided by a mate with a hatchet taken to the deadeyes and lanyards to progressively dismast her. When this peril was over, she could be re-rigged at least partly and often wholly from the spare spars and canvas, etc. always carried. The original *Dunbrody* was probably given hemp standing rigging. Steel wire rigging began to be fitted to such ships within a few years of her launch and we have given it to our ship in the interests of reliability and reduced maintenance and do not feel that it is an anachronism. We retain the deadeyes and lanyards, however, and some ability to cut the masts free.

Compare this with our modern ships who have auxiliary engines, for excellent reasons of course, and who do not therefore need to crowd on the last square inch of sail. We have wire rigging and bottle screws and therefore cannot cut down our rigs in an emergency and need to design for the whole ship and rig to emerge undamaged from a knockdown. This sounds so reasonable that we might wonder why the great age of sailing ships had not thought of it. One reason may be that the amount of ballast required would quite adversely affect the ship motion of a full bodied cargo-carrying hull. The sharp roll, which it would produce, would be dangerous for the rig aloft and affect the drive from the sails.

A feature of the rig which may be worth a comment is that all the upper yards are lowering and may be compared with many of the modern vessels which set fixed yards. Moving yards are more complex both in rigging and in operation but reflect what we choose to think as a superior approach to the use of square rig. Perhaps the greatest benefit comes from the ability partly to lower the yard while the sail is set, allowing it to kite somewhat to reduce heel and improve the wind flow through the yard slots. Another benefit is that it allows the reefing of squaresails. This brings up another aspect of the rig of this kind of ship. They have large topsails in the traditional manner. The decline of revenues brought on by the competition of steam brought with it a decline in crew num-

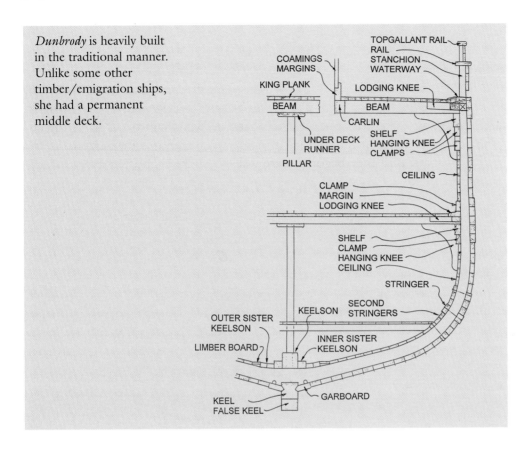

Dunbrody is heavily built in the traditional manner. Unlike some other timber/emigration ships, she had a permanent middle deck.

bers and a need to reduce some of the work about the ship. Split topsails became commonplace and we have made provision in our *Dunbrody* for split topsails to allow for any economic changes during her lifetime.

One final word about that great long bowsprit and jibboom. The centre of pressure of the hull hydrofoil moves forward as hull speed increases until it is right at her shoulders. The ship can only then be balanced by headsails and in turn the more such headsails can be set the more of the main propulsion canvas can be set.

Construction

We have the contract specifications for two similar ships also built in Quebec about the same time as *Dunbrody* and most likely of similar build. There is nothing second rate or cost cutting in them. Further, they were built under the supervision of a ship's Captain, usually to be the first master. We could, therefore, assume that our reconstruction should also demonstrate a good quality of build on the grounds of historical accuracy alone. Of course there were also greater pressures towards quality for our *Dunbrody*. She would in effect represent the Irish nation to the world and especially to the descendants worldwide of emigrants who ever voyaged in any of the emigrant ships.

The method of construction was well documented in various books on naval architecture and construction from the middle of the nineteenth century. Typical scantlings were noted and could be cross checked with the early requirements of Lloyd's Register and even with the wreck of the *Jhellum*, a somewhat similar ship surveyed in the Falklands by a team from Liverpool Maritime Museum. For us to check such scantlings with our own strength calculations was somewhat unnecessary but just added to our confidence.

The construction is classic, with a keel and keelson, built up frames planked inside and out and all clasped together with heavy beams. The timbers employed had to be varied from those which might have made up the original ship. This was partly because they were not available and partly with an eye to the future for a hull which should last a hundred years (with loving care). She was given the benefit of a greenheart keel and keelson and used opepe for the stem and sternpost. The frames were classical oak and she was planked with iroko garboards, Scottish larch and Irish-grown Douglas fir.

Early discussions centred on where she might be built and then we all realised that in New Ross itself there was a derelict shipyard not that many years out of business. Inspection revealed a shallow dry dock. Digging out the mud turned it into a fine deep dock and an admirable site for such a construction, and one from where she could be floated out in due course. Other discussions followed on who might be found with the formidable skills necessary to build a wooden ship of this size. Fortunately Michael Kennedy hove on the scene and assembled a suitable team of shipwrights imbued with a sense of pride and national purpose in their ship. The tented house they built to cover the lofting floor would have graced any glossy magazine on architecture. The scaffolding around their work was both extensive and charming and the suggestion that it should have been varnished was just on the edge of seriousness. Their steam plant would have driven an express train to Dublin and the bending frame, which they used for the steam bending, would have graced a minor cathedral. It may be bathetic to mention it but the bacon butties served at the ten o'clock break were equally magnificent. All concerned with the project clearly were giving of their best.

Inside the enveloping staging the ship grew in strength and grace. An ever-increasing stream of tourists came to see her, boding well for her future as an ambassador for Ireland. She was also being monitored by the Irish authorities. It is not the easiest of tasks to apply modern passenger ship standards to sailing ships, never mind to antique reconstructions. We have designed sailing ships for many countries and many authorities but must hand the palm to the Irish authorities for their attention to detail.

Cutty Sark

The clipper ship at Greenwich

19th Century

Dimensions		
Sparred length	280.00 feet	85.30 metres
Hull length	224.00 feet	68.30 metres
Hull beam	36.00 feet	11.00 metres
Draft	20.00 feet	6.10 metres
Sail area	32,800 square feet	3,047 square metres
Displacement	2,100 tons	
Construction	Iron/wood	
Crew	24–28	

It is with some pleasure that I sneak this ship into the list for my acquaintance with her is of the slenderest. I have always admired the cutaway drawing of her by Max Millar, done years ago for *Yachting World* magazine. My claim to the coat tails of his fame is that I was working for him at the time. Not only did I get to carry his sketching folio but I also got to pencil in the rigging on a cover sheet for him to transfer to the final drawing. Any mistakes, therefore, are to be laid at my door, but I would just say how carefully I proceeded and mention frequent visits to the Nepean Longridge model of *Cutty Sark* in the Science Museum. My drawing board lamp in his office was square rigged for a fortnight while I figured out how it all worked.

Before parting from the subject of Max Millar (that is Millar with an 'a' for those whose thoughts may have strayed to the 'cheeky chappie') I would like to pay a tribute to his genius in illustrating technical subjects. He invented what we now call the cutaway drawing but this was only a tool towards pen and ink drawing explanations of intricate engineering of every subject. His actual pen work was superb, as can be seen in the *Cutty Sark* drawing, and he has never been surpassed in the explanation of engineering, both overall and in detail.

To revert to the actual ship, which I visit frequently and had the impertinence once to board to give a talk on square rig, I think my first impressions were with her human scale. Her beauty is daunting from outboard but once on deck you can see that she did not require the supermen of sailing fiction to drive her. The other matter, not so easily seen these days, was the perfection of her

The Cutty Sark

Max Millar's cutaway drawing of *Cutty Sark*, the historic clipper ship preserved at Greenwich. DRAWING REPRODUCED BY KIND PERMISSION OF *YACHTING WORLD* © 1954.

framing. You only get one shot at bending wrought iron frames when they emerge from the furnace, for they will not go back in again. Any unfairness in the framing can be detected by sighting along the longitudinal stringers which have to dip or rise to accommodate it. I think there are only three frames on one side of the ship and four on the other which vary a tiny bit from perfection.

The clipper ship era, say 1840 to 1870, was short lived and lively and in many ways echoed the time of the cowboys in the Wild West. It would make much better films but clipper ships are probably more expensive than horses and cattle.

Clipper ships were designed to carry light cargoes half-way around the world as fast as possible and in competition, using established and often strong wind systems. Ships before them and other ships sailing beside them were planned for load carrying and adequate functioning in light winds but more for safety in high winds. The clippers were built and manned to the highest technical standards probably in the whole history of merchant shipping. Clouds of sail were set and ships were driven hard and designers were able to explore speed.

The fine bow, the clipper bow, was a major historical novelty which reduced the resistance of a hull especially when driven fast into a seaway. The bow surfaces also gave admirable steering control which allowed the master to maximise the windward performance. The thin bow had to be allied with hull length to reduce pitching and diving, and sailing ship proportions sprang away from the past.

The shape of the stern began to control the potential passage speed. There were two main stern form types. One was fine with smooth up-turning buttocks and this reduced the skin area and hull drag in the middle order of conditions. However, if the ship was overdriven this kind of stern could suck down and lead to pooping. The other stern form was much fuller underwater with little tendency to suck down at speed. The former was preferred for what was probably the most critical speeds, between eight and twelve knots, representing performance in the twenty to thirty knot wind speed bands. The fuller stern could be driven with greater safety up to the normal maximum hull speed of the order of twenty knots. This would only normally be accessed in winds of forty to fifty knots but might be attractive to some hard driving captains. *Cutty Sark*, which has a quite powerful stern, was especially noted for her hard wind performances in the southern latitudes.

There is one myth about the clippers that needs to be put in context. I have heard it said that they were designed and used for blasting downwind in the trades and roaring forties and not much use to windward. This ignores the fact that the clippers had, for instance, to get to windward against the south westerlies to leave Europe and had a great deal of windward work in the China Sea. It is likely that, as in modern racing, ability to windward was the key to success.

T.S. Royalist

The Sea Cadets' brig

1971

Dimensions

Sparred length	99.00 feet	30.20 metres
Hull length	76.00 feet	23.20 metres
Waterline length	60.00 feet	18.30 metres
Beam	20.00 feet	6.10 metres
Draft	8.50 feet	2.60 metres
Working sail area	4,315 square feet	400 square metres
Displacement	80 tons	
Construction	Steel	
Crew	6	
Cadets	26	

The Project

Quite often we meet the nicest of people who, in conversation, mention that some relative of theirs was largely responsible for *Royalist*. No doubt they were in it somewhere and we are delighted with their identification and allegiance. We know, however, that *Royalist* was the concept and achievement of one man – Morin Scott. For proof, should it ever be needed, we can point out who paid for some of the early drawings. We know a great deal more than that, we know of his enthusiasm. We know of his extraordinary hard work to convince the world that a square rigged ship with (as some perceived) its associations with dangerous working aloft and a hard life on deck was just where every mum would be happy to send her young cadet child. It was an extraordinary *tour-de-force*, but Morin demonstrated the ideal with other smaller sailing ships and cajoled and convinced until money appeared and the ship was built.

Amazing as it was in 1971, there is another aspect of this kind of project for which Morin has an undoubted genius. That is to get the size and style of a project right. This may seem simple but as every designer knows it is possibly the most difficult thing to get right. Size bears on every other feature of a cadet ship – particularly cost and revenue – but more than anything on its ability to attract those who are to use it. In this case it was to be a ship for sea cadets which

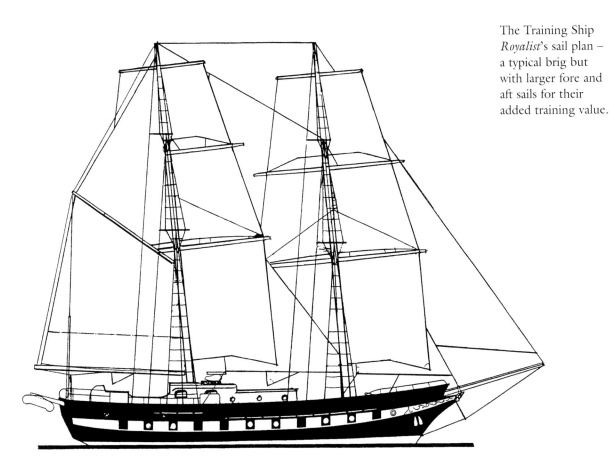

The Training Ship *Royalist*'s sail plan – a typical brig but with larger fore and aft sails for their added training value.

would not be the same ship that you might design for adults. It was also Morin who took us further through the novelty of square rig and who insisted that not only will square riggers sail well but that *Royalist* really had to do so.

The first barrier, as we saw it at the time, to getting the ship efficiently to windward was her square yards. Other square riggers we looked at seemed to have given up the struggle and could only brace their yards to some forty degrees from the centreline, this bracing angle being limited when the yards come hard against the shrouds and backstays. We knew, especially from Fincham's classic book of 1854, that bracing to thirty degrees was quite usual in the great age of square riggers and so, with John Powell's Sparlight company (then the foremost aluminium masts and spar makers) we set about achieving this. Next we rigged her more or less with a competent rig of fore and aft sails as well. This, we argued to ourselves, would provide valuable additional training for the cadets and would be useful if the ship had to motor/sail to meet her schedules at any time.

With the sail power unit optimised as far as we could take it, the next thing to look at was the windward ability of the hull. She was, in historical terms, very lightly loaded having only her engines and cadets to carry in place of a full load of cargo or armaments. The sailing cargo ship used her complete hull as a very large hydrofoil of, by yacht standards, very shallow proportions and an exceptionally

107

OPPOSITE: The Sea Cadet brig *T.S. Royalist* in the Parade of Sail in Penzance Bay in 1996. PHOTO: MAX

slow relative water flow speed. With *Royalist*'s displacement the hull hydrofoil would be so shallow as to severely limit its windward ability. We lost no time over this and adopted, for the same reasons as yachts of this century, a protruding keel form to take us to windward.

There was another reason for this, of possibly greater importance. The ship was required by Morin and her owners to be self-righting from a knockdown. This is now a basic regulatory requirement for all commercial sailing ships. If you ballast a conventional sailing ship hull form, especially one on the shallow side, to achieve the self-righting such ballasting will produce a very sharp roll in normal service. Such sharp rolling would not only be hard on the gear aloft but even harder on trainees up in the rigging as well as being unpleasant to live with on deck. So again we followed the classic yacht form for the same reasons and gave her a ballast keel at the expense perhaps of some additional draft.

This question of getting the hull motion right for young cadets took quite a great deal of thought. We finally maximised the hull water plane so that she would sail as upright as possible in light winds. Next we softened her general form so that she would roll as gently as possible. With any wind at all we believed she would be wind steadied and this seems to have worked out. It is also pleasing to report that when she once did have a knockdown she popped up again in more or less good order.

We and Morin insisted that the old seagoing principle of two of everything should be followed as far as possible. When she was new there was some criticism of a sailing ship which had twin engines. They were installed primarily to ensure reliability in the voyage timing. It would be unthinkable to have a joining party of cadets standing on a jetty and no ship to join. Equally unthinkable for parents, possibly having made a long journey, would be to have to stand looking hopefully out to sea for their offspring.

We were somewhat beset by what we might call the shellback tendency about how both the performance and the pure enjoyment of being under sail would be completely ruined by fitting an engine at all, never mind two of them. We had thought those aspects through and made some accommodations for these points of view. First we fitted as much sound absorbents as practical and also underwater exhausts. An engine or engines can be run with the minimum impact on the sailors on deck. This allows, for instance, for the lee engine to be run to pep up the performance in light conditions to maintain schedules. The engines can also be brought quickly into play to complete a manoeuvre should its successful completion be in doubt. Overall, good engine power is totally necessary these days when sail training ships have to operate among the shipping lanes. In terms of drag to spoil the sailing we could point to the fact that, one propeller or two, you needed the same total blade area to drive her and that with twin propellers there is no cross flow through a propeller aperture to stall part of the rudder. There was also some initial muttering about her paint scheme with its gunports. It appeared to some to be an unnecessary obeisance to the past when we were trying to be a modern ship. Morin knew that it would be

attractive in itself but we all realised its value, when she was new, of pointing her out amongst other shipping as a training ship which might, for instance, make unusual and unexpected manoeuvres – and that people could readily recognise her.

Once started *Royalist* positively glowed from good will. She was built in East Cowes at the Groves and Guttridge yard then owned by Charles Gardner and his brother Jimmy, known in boating circles as the owners and drivers of the classic racing powerboat *Surfury*. Our *Royalist* was in fact built within a few miles of that other *Royalist* built for the Charles Brooke who used her for a career in the Far East which finished with him as Rajah of Sarawak. The shipbuilders, one and all, treated the project like a favourite child and many were the special touches and little bits of additional work that went into her construction. We kept a very tight control over the extras as the ship was built but at the time and increasingly so in retrospect we have a suspicion that Charles Gardner treated the ship with a great deal of financial as well as other marks of benevolence. Uffa Fox, then a little elderly, had himself rowed up river to see her launched and Princess Anne named her and has kept an eye on her ship ever since.

We are all particularly pleased when Lloyd's Register under whose survey she had been built gave her the 1971 Award for best design and construction.

Royalist is a firm favourite among our ships. Our personal involvement is so many years back that we think that we can be objective about our enjoyment of her. It all boils down to our appreciation of the Sea Cadet Corps and how they run the ship. The cadets are always clean and disciplined and brimming over with good old-fashioned zeal, every one brave and smart as paint and, in our experience, very well mannered. The Sea Cadet officers run the ship with a quite marvellous combination of authority and compassion. The overall result is a pleasure to see and visit.

There are many anecdotes which illustrate the standards of the ship – possibly all apocryphal but they help to explain our enthusiasm. There is, for example, the mother who is reported as writing to the Offshore Commander: *'I don't know what you did to him in one week that I could not do in fourteen years but he came home and tidied his bedroom.'*

The Lines

This was our first attempt to solve the conundrum of building a ship of a historically commercial type but which would not have to carry a commercial cargo. The historical brig went to windward on her hull shape alone and to optimise this the hull had to be as short and deep as possible. We also had other factors to consider. Although fortunately rare, it is possible for freak wind conditions to flatten a sailing ship until she lies on her beam ends. Historically, ships were planned so that part of the rig would break or could be broken by the crew to relieve the pressure and let her upright again. Modern thinking (and regula-

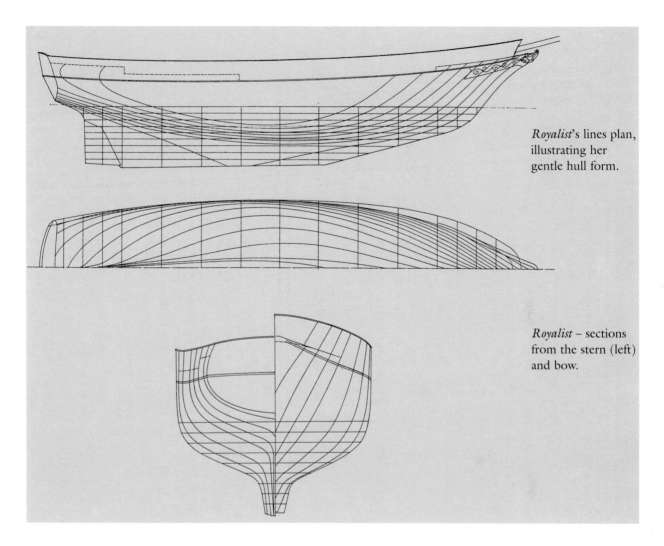

Royalist's lines plan, illustrating her gentle hull form.

Royalist – sections from the stern (left) and bow.

tions) require that self-righting has to occur without any action from the crew whatsoever. The problem of the sharper roll of a suitably balanced traditional hull form is an important consideration. Another factor particular to a square rigged ship is that the crew have a great deal of work to do about the deck and if this is to be done efficiently the normal sailing angle of heel cannot be the extravagant angles with which we are all familiar with the Bermudan yacht. Our solution was to work from the yacht form rather than that of the historical brig. Essentially, we enlarged the floating waterplane to add to her sailing stability, softened the bilges, quite drastically, to soften her rolling motion and added a yacht type keel for windward work and to give the necessary moments for self-righting. We also gave her deep and low buttocks aft for directional stability and to reduce pitching. How it works is something like this. In light winds the ship has good initial stability from her waterplane. When the wind picks up and she heels to some ten degrees she is largely wind-steadied with the ballast keel beginning to have an effect. At a full knockdown the ballast keel is the principal component of the recovery.

T.S. Royalist hard on
the wind, showing
how high a modern
square rigger can
point. PHOTO: MAX

Walk Through

There was considerable pressure to maximise the accommodation within a particular size and cost of ship. However, the deck layout is fairly classical with a large deckhouse and large enclosed cockpit. Such a deckhouse (not immediately accepted by sailors from commercial sail who prefer wide open decks) is an excellent feature of a training ship on several grounds. Not in order of importance, these include lee side and cockpit shelter for cadets working on deck and, said a little under one's breath for such ambitious seamen, shelter for those who may not wish to risk themselves below decks for a little while. The deckhouse itself offers more warmth and shelter to sustain the watch on deck in poor conditions.

We put the large enclosed cockpit into the ship specifically to allow the watch officer to gather his cadets together in some security in really unpleasant conditions. It has always been a source of great pleasure to us that when the ship takes guests to sea on a 'Sunday Sea Day' they are corralled safely in the cockpit out of everyone's way while the cadets get on with running the ship.

T.S. Royalist racing off Milford Haven in the 1991 Cutty Sark Tall Ships' Race.
PHOTO: MAX

113

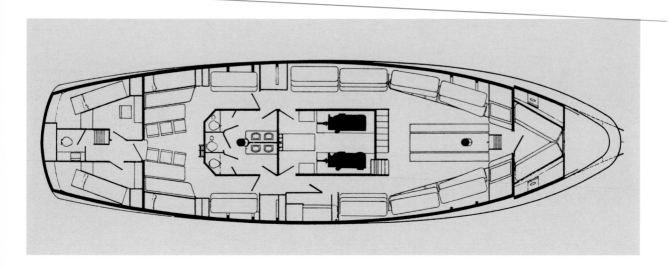

Royalist's below deck arrangement, showing how the various berths are laid out.

As far as possible we like to get two paths to everywhere in the ship. There are two entrances to the cockpit from the deck and two entries to the ship from the cockpit. In fact there is an additional companion entry to the deckhouse chart room because we can reserve one for the navigator while the other leads forward. Next in the deckhouse we fitted a small compartment as a radio room and envisaged the cadets under instruction there as well as in the chart room. This disappeared at the first refit so that the navigator and the radio could be together and also to meet the ever growing demand for more storage space. Next forward again in the lower part of the deckhouse was a small messdeck – primarily planned to accommodate a whole watch for instruction and for getting warm drinks from the galley next door. The alleyway past these compartments was planned to be the path taken by cadets at sea when starting a watch where they could be inspected in the watchroom for oilskins and safety harnesses, etc., before venturing on deck. At the end of their watch they could also pause for a hot drink on their way to their cots should they wish.

The galley is fitted with a large oil-fired marine stove which is marvellous for warming both ship and crew. It also has a serving hatch to the deckhouse alley that leads to the lower deck. Below decks the accommodation is arranged around an island site containing the engines and the washrooms. This arrangement allows quick access around the ship should one access be blocked for any reason. The cadet accommodation is in pipe cots with four of them right forward ahead of the required forward bulkhead. We always said that these should be allocated to the senior cadets because sheer pride would help to reduce the effect of the motion. I can remember Princess Anne giving a look of some disbelief in this happy theory when I had the honour of taking her round the ship.

The big forecastle with its large table is the real centre of the ship and is where the cadets eat and tell tall stories and write their postcards from foreign ports. In recent years we have had to introduce another bulkhead across the ship at the forward end of the engine room to meet new regulations but this has been done without much affecting the general feel of the ship.

The aft accommodation (from aft) includes a very respectable cabin for the Captain and a not quite so large a one for the first officer and they have their own washroom right aft where it is tempting to observe that such seamen should be able to withstand the motion. Nowadays it is odd that we are much more conscious of protocol and would inevitably port for starboard this area to house the Captain to starboard.

The aft accommodation has a direct companion to the aft of the cockpit to allow the quickest attendance on deck should it be required and there is also a direct access from the wardroom to the chart house. This is obstructed for normal use by some added furnishings but remains for the passage of commands and emergency use.

Forward of the wardroom and housed in the aft end of the island site is the cadets' washroom. This has three WC/shower compartments and four washbasins to serve some twenty persons. When the ship was being planned one of her supporters was of the opinion that there must be plenty of showers and hot water as *'the boys will undoubtedly want to shower when they come off watch'*. Morin Scott's response was: *'Shower! – It's difficult enough to get them to clean their teeth!'*

The machinery room contains two 130 hp Perkins engines plus the generators. These latter indicate the biggest change in sailing ship fit-out during the life of *Royalist*. When we designed her we had to argue long and strong to get a tiny AC generator set into her. We cunningly left space for more and larger generators. From a condition when every true seaman once sucked his teeth whenever the generator was started, current ships can now rarely run without a continuous and copious supply of AC electricity.

Of course much has changed in the ship during her life and one can point to and appreciate all manner of improvements. Not least the wardroom facilities for entertaining guests which now has a well filled cups and trophies locker.

The Rig

This is a classic brig rig and perhaps the interest is in the detail and the performance. She has proved to be suitable for training young cadets. The sail areas and rigging loads are not so big or heavy as to inhibit them driving their ship up to its limits with apparent confidence. In general, a crew newly joined on a Saturday is showing off to guests on Sunday in inshore waters and sailing to foreign parts on Monday.

The solid wooden climbing frames fitted to the shrouds in place of rope ladder type ratlines take the eye. The principal reason for these is

These sketches illustrate the various strands of opinion represented in the *Royalist* design committee. From top: the sailing men, the warship group, the parade ground tendency, the publicity department, and the perfectionists.

T.S. Royalist on yard trials in the Solent following her 1992 refit. Note the red ensign in place of her normal blue one. PHOTO: MAX

safety. With cadets climbing aloft, many for the very first time, the wooden framing makes for a much more confident climb and from the point of view of the instructors the rungs are very much more durable and very much less likely to get damaged. An experienced crew always inspect rope ratlines every time they pass and cut any of which they are in doubt to be replaced as soon as practical. This is not to be expected of newly joined crew members. Another advantage is that the vertical wooden framing acts somewhere between a guide and protection from chafe for the running rigging in the area.

Not quite so obvious is that *Royalist* is fitted with the traditional, and we believe seamanlike, hoisting yards unlike some other modern ships who use fixed yards. Hoisting yards makes for more work for the crew on deck but allow, we think, squaresails to be set more efficiently and also allows them to be fitted for reefing.

Royalist has a good performance to windward, pointing some fifty degrees either side of the true wind. One of the sights we have treasured was to see her

cruising up and down the line at the start of the race from Falmouth to Lisbon in 1982 under the command of Commander David Gay, a well known ocean racing helmsman and a previous sailing master of the Royal yacht *Bloodhound*. He roared her along, catching many competitors on the starboard tack until at the moment of the starting gun he hardened her up on the wind, crossed the line at full speed ahead of everyone and, some eight hundred miles later, beat the whole fleet to first place on handicap.

Sea cadets changing sail as *Royalist* races with *Malcolm Miller*. PHOTO: MAX

T.S. Varuna

Royalist's sister ship

1979

Dimensions

Sparred length	99.00 feet	30.20 metres
Hull length	76.00 feet	23.20 metres
Waterline length	60.00 feet	18.30 metres
Beam	20.00 feet	6.10 metres
Draft	8.50 feet	2.60 metres
Displacement	80 tons	
Working sail area	4,315 square feet	400 square metres
Construction	Steel	
Crew	6	
Cadets	26	

The Indian Sea Cadet brig *Varuna*'s nameplate. Varuna is an Indian god: 'Lord of physical and moral order'.
PHOTO: ROSEMARY MUDIE

*V*aruna is a sister ship to *Royalist*, built in India from the same plans with spars, sails and rigging supplied from England from the same manufacturers. She too was built for sea cadets and operated in a manner similar to *Royalist* for many years. She too was painted with the gun port livery as her sister ship but as befits a hot climate ship it was reversed with a white hull, which we very much admired.

The Indian Navy borrowed her from the Indian Sea Cadet Corps to represent India in the Australian Bicentennial and sent her there on her own bottom. In itself this was a considerable undertaking for a small ship. When crossing the Great Australian Bight they discovered a crack developing at the foot of the foremast. With amazing seamanship they got the broken mast overboard together with the now unsupported second mast. It must have been very well done because it was accomplished with the minimum of damage to the ship and not a scratch to any of the officers and cadets.

They motored the ship on to Adelaide and we all set to to find her a new rig in short order so that she could still make the parade of sail in Sydney. Fortunately, it was not long since Australia had hosted the America's Cup event and there were spare masts and sails from the twelve metre yachts to be had. She appeared in Sydney with a smart schooner rig and probably only the most knowledgeable were aware that this was not how she started from India.

Unfortunately, attempts to re-rig her again as a brig failed, probably, we understand, on the basis of the costs involved. She is still sailing around as a schooner and there are still plans to re-rig her as a brig on that happy day when the funds come in.

S.T.S. Lord Nelson

The barque everyone can sail in

1985

Dimensions			
Sparred length		169.50 feet	51.70 metres
Hull length		141.00 feet	42.98 metres
Waterline length		122.00 feet	37.19 metres
Beam		28.00 feet	8.53 metres
Draft		13.50 feet	4.12 metres
Displacement		400 tons	406.40 kilos
Sail area		10,755 square feet	1,000 square metres
Construction	Steel		
Crew	10		
Voyage crew	40		

The Project

Chris Rudd is one of those amazing people who actually change the world for the better. In the 1980s he took both able and disabled youngsters inshore sailing in his own boat and he did not see any justice when the able-bodied went on to sail offshore while the disabled young could not. He applied for a grant from the Queen's Silver Jubilee Fund and set about changing the situation. The Jubilee Sailing Trust was the result and he organised a small but high-powered committee with suitable expertise. Originally, their ambition lay with something like a Thames barge. Fortunately Morin Scott was a member of this committee (see *Royalist*) and he was able to point out that there were two criteria for the new ship under discussion to be successful. First, that there had to be a great deal of work in sailing the ship so that everyone onboard was part of the sailing team. In any ordinary Thames barge or Bermudan rigged vessel the work required very few but reasonably skilled crew. The able-bodied would then very kindly do the work for the disabled. His second point was equally practical – crew in wheelchairs must be able to pass each other on deck or a vital crew response might become delayed. He also added that it would not be unreasonable for the normal sailing angle of the ship to be less than the angle at which a wheelchair capsizes. Morin assessed that the ship that would best suit Chris

OPPOSITE: The Sail Training Ship *Lord Nelson* is unique in being the first sail training ship in the world designed for both able-bodied and disabled voyage crews. PHOTO: MAX

121

Rudd's objectives would therefore have to be at least thirty metres in length and be square rigged. He suggested an order of costs for such a ship and it is rumoured that at least one member of the committee resigned on the spot.

The early years of the project were largely educational. The medical members of the committee set about teaching the rest of us the facts of life for those with various disabilities and not just those in wheelchairs. At the same time various able and disabled volunteers put in actual sea time onboard the square riggers *Royalist* and *Marques,* neither of which had any special provision for any disabilities whatsoever. I think we were all, medical department included, quite astonished at the outcomes. In a quite biblical manner people got out of wheelchairs and others even quite forgot where they had left their crutches. Some discovered abilities within themselves, both physical and mental, of which they had long despaired, when faced with the inspiration of a vivid and attractive new environment. Also, and this was as big a factor as the effect on some disabled, the able began to forget that the disabled were a different group. One lady matron, overtaken by seasickness, took considerable pleasure in being helped below by one of her erstwhile charges. We found that our best helmsman was a young man not allowed by his disabilities to drive a car and that the blind were more at home aloft than many, if not most, of the sighted. In fact everything that Chris had been hoping and planning was, to his team, thoroughly proven.

The rest of the world took longer to catch on. The Jubilee Sailing Trust in its early days was fairly thoroughly beset by not just unbelievers but by those who thought that we were being downright wicked in taking disabled people to sea. The definitive answer came from Dr. Tony Hicklin, the chief medical member of the Trust. *'We are not TAKING disabled people to sea but making it possible for them to come if they want to.'* Those who could support us, very often out of sheer concern for the wellbeing of this different race of people called the disabled, often proposed the most extensive and often cumbersome equipment for the new ship which by then was taking shape on the drawing board. Our favourite was that the ship should have a fully watertight deckhouse in which the disabled would gather *when* (our italics) the ship sank. They would fire off a series of explosive securing bolts and float clear of the ship (presumably waving a sad farewell to their drowning shipmates as they went). It was a protective and kindly meant thought very typical of a normal approach to disabilities before Chris worked his revolution in public attitudes.

The ship when we first laid her out was to be a barque of some 135 feet in length and her design went forward as the Jubilee Sailing Trust chartered and adapted the brigantine *Soren Larsen* to run a trial season. The major adaptation made to her was to fit a wheelchair lift from deck to the cabin space below and to fit out some cabins and washrooms to disabled accommodation standards. She proved that there was a full market for such sailing from both able and disabled and was, if it was necessary, the final confirmation that Chris Rudd had been right. We all then settled down to getting on with the new ship.

It will come as little surprise to hear that this ship presented the Trust with

two major problems. It will be even less surprising to hear that the first lay in raising the wind for her. The original tranche of Silver Jubilee money was quite small – aimed at feasibility studies and research rather than shipbuilding. So virtually the whole cost of a new ship of some four hundred tons had to be funded and this took what might be called a very great deal of effort. Friends and supporters rallied round and money started to come in although not initially in ship-building quantities. Charles Munro made a painting of the ship so that prints might be sold for funds and this turned out to be a mainspring in our first really major donation: from the Beaverbrook Foundation. This reflected support from Sir Max Aitken who was by then a wheelchair user himself. Other organisations also produced handsome contributions but money continued to be a problem. The chief moneyman on the committee, a very distinguished international financier, once declared that we could only build her on a mortgage over his dead body. Well we did, he retained his health, and the mortgage was paid off out of earnings before the full term.

A fundraising painting by Charles Munro of the original 'Jubilee' barque, at 135 foot length and with a smaller rig. The very deep courses reflect the thinking at that time that they would have to be handled by power winches. Her size was increased to accommodate a larger number of professional crew.

The other problem was equally predictable. The Department of Transport is no doubt ace with steamships and healthy crews but fell into a major wobbly when we talked about building the biggest square rigger for many years and manning it with, amongst others, ladies and gentlemen in wheelchairs together with the blind, deaf and elderly. The Trust even paid for a representative of the Department to join the design committee and there was no aspect of the ship as planned on paper, long before she was built, of which they were not aware and for which we thought we had their approval.

O tempores o mores. The ship was planned for a complement of twenty able-bodied and twenty disabled together with, initially, a permanent crew of eight. The disabled group was to include up to eight in wheelchairs and planning was to be on the basis that every disabled person would have an allocated able buddy to work with. Special provision was made for all the physically disabled who would come onboard but there is no doubt that provision for wheelchairs was a mainspring of the design. Space for them to get around was principally a problem of space planning. Getting them into and out of the ship was more difficult as maritime regulations require a high coaming or sill at every entrance to stop any water on deck getting inside. These are mandatory and, of course, a 300 or 450 millimetre sill poses an insuperable problem to a wheelchair. A ramp might do ashore but it would either be perilous or take up too much deck space afloat. Our solution was to fit flush entries with two sets of watertight doors separated by a fully drained compartment. We also added hinged coamings which could be brought into play in an emergency. Space for wheelchairs had to be kept to the minimum. The limbless, those unsteady on their feet and the blind would be better supported afloat by narrow alleyways with good handrails. The Trust experimented with tracking systems for wheelchairs. An experimental set-up was popular on the *Soren Larsen* trials, especially for wheelchair racing in harbour. A wide range of attachment systems and special chairs, some powered, were proposed, discussed and eventually discarded. It was clear that all occupants vastly preferred the chair they were used to and on a bigger ship a free chair was found to be practical with only a need for anchor points in special places such as at the chart table. One notable piece of equipment is the helm chair which is tracked and articulated so that everyone can find some arrangement which suits them when steering the ship.

When we started the design in 1978 it was thought that, as in other ships of that time, we were really dealing with males with perhaps a few ladies for whom some cabin accommodation would suffice. We even had provision for the crew washrooms to be divided if it should be required into M and F rather than offering division from the start. By the time the ship was finishing another social revolution had revolved and it was clear that not only were we talking a fifty-fifty division in those coming to join the ship but that they could all now sleep together – that is, in the same sleeping accommodation. Only washrooms retained their modesty but we had to add a pair right forward so that nobody had to pass through the main saloon on a night call.

Eventually we increased the size of the ship to some 43 metres in length and put her construction out to tender. The Wivenhoe Shipyard took her on with enthusiasm and built her with great pride and generous workmanship. She was launched by Lady Aitken and positively roared into the river displaying, we all said, enthusiasm for the work ahead. Unfortunately the yard went down over a different contract and equally unfortunately the JST had not thought it necessary to cover the contract with a performance bond. Things might have been extremely awkward at that stage but the money situation was resolved although remaining difficult. The ship was then towed round to Vosper Thornycroft at Southampton for her major completion and E. Cole & Sons up the Medina river for the final work.

At this stage it is necessary to bring the Department of Transport back into the saga. They run a system where each individual surveyor has to sign personally for the safety of the ship to which he has been allocated. Special ships like *Lord Nelson* do not fit exactly into international regulations and a great deal of detail is left to the discretion of the man on the spot. Approvals we thought that we had from head office in London (and approvals we certainly had from the Wivenhoe surveyor who was a member of the design committee) did not transfer to Southampton.

Lord Nelson head on, showing the full stack of the foremast squaresails.

The view at Southampton was that a disabled crew could not be accepted as anything but virtual passengers, and to be fair that was not an uncommon reaction at that stage. However, with the ship nearly completed, as much of the Passenger Ship Load Line regulations as possible began to be applied. Different minds have differing views on even minor details and the consequent reworking and respecifying costed us all time and money. It became imperative to get the ship finished and into revenue earning service as soon as possible. We were very fortunate that Vosper Thornycroft had taken the ship on. They were able to keep technical discipline going in a fast moving completion and the warship standards used for her systems have stood her in excellent stead ever since.

One moment to treasure was when the masts were stepped. So many faces were pressed to the shipyard windows overlooking the event that they looked like jars of pickled onions. Harry Spencer's riggers, every one as if a practised thespian, played to this gallery. Stepping tall masts is not that easy but they put on a show of the utmost casualness with orders conveyed with no more than a lift of an eyebrow or at most a forefinger.

We discovered that the permanent crew would be required to demonstrate that they would be able to handle the ship themselves under full sail and would

Lord Nelson's transom badge carved by Norman Gaches.
PHOTO: MAX

be examined with full sail set in all the normal evolutions of a sailing ship, and in the confined waters of the Solent. This took us a bit aback as we had anticipated and planned that when the crew were, as it were, short-handed, the ship would be snugged down to match and increasing use made of the engines. Our steamship men did not see it that way; perhaps they were only interested in the simple steamship type concept of full power trials. This was one of the reasons why we had to add an additional pair of permanent crew, making them up to ten. I may add that on this official trial the permanent crew did everything quite magnificently with cook, engineer and medical purser as active on deck as the boatswain and his mates and all under the command of Captain Mark Kemmis Betty sailing his very first barque. They could not be failed.

The ship in service has been a success due as much as anything to her succeeding crews over the years. Those who have not sailed in her before, both able and disabled, join with some nervousness. The crew turn them into a ship family within twenty-four hours. Like any family no one is expected to perform feats obviously beyond their capacity but when they do, and it is quite often, the whole crew are delighted.

With due modesty we can report that she has won both British and Italian design awards and has run at better than ninety per cent occupancy throughout her life. She has cruised across the Atlantic and currently runs a winter programme around the Canary Islands. She commonly sails in company with the tall ships fleets in their races but usually does not take part in the racing because of the age restrictions (half the race crew have to be between fifteen and twenty-five). However, with fifty per cent of the crew of the appropriate ages, she is to take part in the Tall Ships 2000 races across the Atlantic and back.

The Lines

Two major and strongly held opposing points of view were put to us in the early days. First was that we should consider a novel ship for the novel crew who were to man her. This attitude tipped towards a catamaran style of craft which, by sailing upright, would better suit the wheelchair crew. The other faction, and one with which we quickly identified, was that we should be planning a vessel as close as possible in appearance and operation to all the other tall ships. Above all it was thought to be important that we did not finish up with a 'ghetto' vessel where our crew might be seen to belong to a different group to the others. At least part of our concern about the catamaran concept was that it would be difficult to plan one with the softness of motion required, both for the rig and the crew.

The requirements for the hull of *Lord Nelson* in any case mirrored and exaggerated those for *Royalist*. After some ten or fifteen years of experience with her we had every reason to feel that we were on the right track. We could therefore consider a next generation in terms of improvements and developments. In addition to the soft roll it was important to keep the normal sailing angle under control and inside the capsizing angle of the average wheelchair. The Royal Navy had a hydraulic rolling deck at Gosport where they checked equipment

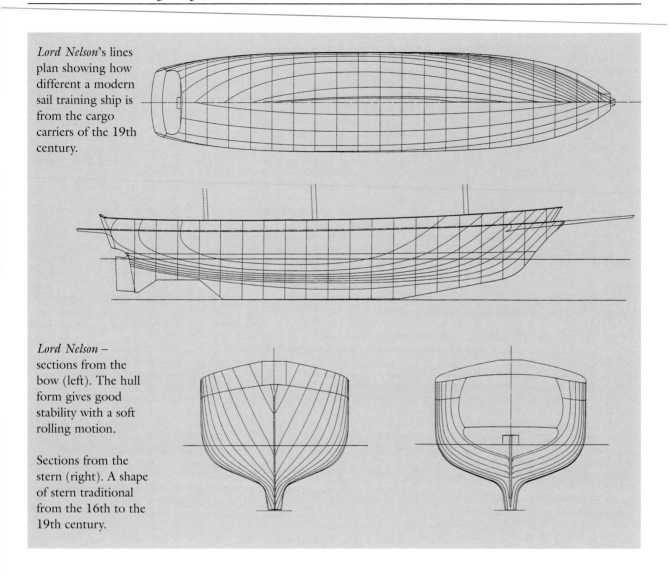

Lord Nelson's lines plan showing how different a modern sail training ship is from the cargo carriers of the 19th century.

Lord Nelson – sections from the bow (left). The hull form gives good stability with a soft rolling motion.

Sections from the stern (right). A shape of stern traditional from the 16th to the 19th century.

and a natural first act was to take some volunteers along in their wheelchairs and try to capsize them. We found that they started to tip at about twelve degrees and therefore took a figure of some ten degrees as our mark. Incidentally this is the same angle which is regarded as a limit for elderly passengers when evacuating a passenger ship in an emergency.

We therefore planned her with the maximum waterplane area. Instead of a full counter stern, as *Royalist*, we drew up an immersed transom and in fact we had to do so anyway to be out of balance with the full bow form to reduce the build up of synchronous pitching. The full bow is valuable in helping to reduce the burying of the bow under the moment of the high rig which carries sail substantially higher than any schooner. The full bow also improves the hydrofoil work of the hull when making to windward although, as in *Royalist*, part of this is effected by the ballast keel.

The hull was tank-tested by the Wolfson Unit at Southampton and they, quite properly, said that the hull resistance at certain parts of the speed range would be reduced if we shaped the stern more like *Royalist*. However, we had other fish to fry, we wanted initial stability and reduced pitching and were more than satisfied with the trade off. It was very interesting how the logic of this approach resulted in a stern form commonly found in the ships of the eighteenth and nineteenth centuries.

Another priority lay in the possibility of a slower reaction time by the crew when the ship was being manoeuvred. To improve the speed of manoeuvre we shortened the ballast keel and fitted her with a skeg so that she should be able to turn easily and quickly when required.

In her early days at sea we had reports that she was 'only just directionally stable' and that some found her difficult to steer. There were all manners of discussion and views. We started with the advantage of knowing that there was nothing novel in the hull form and that it must therefore be something else. A close analysis of the problem quickly revealed the answer. Because the ship, being considerably larger, normally sailed at a much lower relative speed than the other sailing vessels with this hull form she did in fact have a rudder problem. The yacht-type rudder we had fitted was not 'biting' until it left the water shadow of the skeg to which it was faired. No reaction to the helm could be noticed until some three or four degrees were put on, when the ship, suddenly feeling a fair amount of helm, began to swing fast. The solution, interestingly enough, had been in front of us in that all the sailing ships of yore used thick rudders with squared off trailing edges without any fairing. This not only gives an instant response to a very small helm angle, but by inducing air down the back of the rudder both reduces resistance and increases its effect. In fact we just added a bit of extra plate area on the trailing edge which seems to have done the trick.

Walk Through

The layout of the ship was originally planned on the basis that wheelchair crews should have full access to all those parts of the ship to which they might wish to go on pleasure or on duty. In our early idealism it was even thought that one day we might see at least one wheelchair user amongst the permanent crew. The next criterion was that the whole crew including those in wheelchairs should be able

The below decks layout of *Lord Nelson*. The eight cabins amidships are specially planned for crew in wheelchairs.

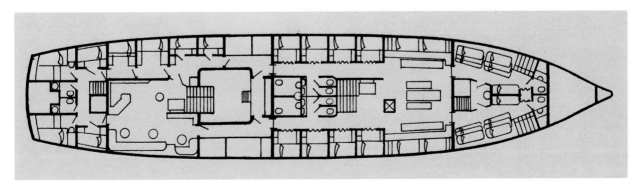

to evacuate the ship in short order. To this end every part of the hull which would be sealed by watertight doors in the event of an accident was given a power chair lift backed up with a block and tackle. Noting that maritime regulations forbade the use of closed lifts on such occasions in case the occupants got trapped by a power failure, we were encouraged to fit open topped lifts in the forward and aft compartments and powered them from a large bank of sealed batteries in case the generators were not running. At the time of planning this we understood that it had DTp approval, but this turned out to be something of an illusion. On the other hand they allowed us to fit deep windows in the forward deckhouse so that those in wheelchairs could see out to the horizon and came forward with generosity in several other areas to meet the objectives of the ship.

For general wheelchair access about the ship we initially fitted these two vertical lifts together with wheelchair platform lifts on the main companions. We also fitted the main companions with a pair of seat lifts for the non-wheelchair users who might not be too steady on the stairs.

On deck we were happy to fit substantial deckhouses for the shelter they give the crew at sea as well as the economical space they add to the construction. The forward deckhouse contains one of the main entries to the ship, wheelchair lavatories to port and a large and drained lobby for oilskins to starboard. Forward of that is the galley and an on-deck messroom. The galley is divided into a hot galley where the professional cook can wrestle with a powerful and very hot stove and a cold galley which is a food preparation and snack area with a food lift to the main mess in the deck below. The hot galley is divided off and, considered perilous to the unsteady, is not accessible or available for use by any other than the official cook. The rest can use the cold galley at any time of day or night for the hot drinks and small snacks without which life at sea is apparently unbearable. The cold galley is open to a small messroom planned to accommodate a whole watch accoutred and ready for action in bad weather and has the aforesaid deep windows so that the wheelchair element can see out without stretching. It is large enough for a whole watch to eat together. At the fore end was one of the vertical lifts to the lower deck, but this has now been removed.

The after deckhouse is the other main entry to the ship and has a deck lavatory on the starboard side. With that in the forward deckhouse there is a deck lavatory suitable for disabled crew to leeward on either tack. On the other side is an access lobby and lift to the charthouse. In between this area and the after part of the house is a raised chart room and cockpit with a large store under. This store was originally planned for the storage of ship's wheelchairs but is now used for almost everything else. The aft end is what the Americans would call 'Captain's country'. It consists of an on-deck stateroom and 'en suite'. We intended it to be generous for his rest but more than usually in touch with what is going on about the ship on deck. It is perhaps not completely fair for the resting aspect as we put the helm position immediately on top of his cabin. It is here that the voices of alarm are raised first, usually with the clear and penetrating note of concern that has a captain on deck in his pyjamas in short order.

The half-height cockpit is both a workstation for the mizzenmast and something of a sheltered area completely under the eye of the crew in the chart room. This latter is set up as an alternative and interior steering position. Those coming on steering watch come up from the main deck by lift or companion stairs to the charthouse. There they can be briefed before making their way aft and up to the helm. The advantage of having the charthouse forward of and below the helm is that the doors can usually be left open and orders easily given to those on watch at the helm.

From the main entry in the forward deckhouse there is a broad companion and both wheel and chair lifts to the lower deck mess. This is the main dining and social area of the ship and food is brought down and cleared by means of a dumb waiter type lift. In principle, nobody sleeps in this space but pressures of commerce required the fitting of some four pilot berths against the shipside for

A general view of *Lord Nelson* sailing off the east coast of Scotland.
PHOTO: MAX

131

boatswain's mates – a sterling group who work about twenty-five hours a day for no pay. Ahead of this is the main dormitory-type sleeping area with a pair of night conveniences at the fore end. Here the voyage crew sleep in pipe cots which can be folded up during the day to increase the airspace.

Aft of this there is a technical island with pump rooms and washrooms on the centreline, again with a disabled standard washroom to port and starboard to make for better access on either tack. Outboard of the island are four cabins each side designed for the use of wheelchair crew and their helpers. The island principle carries on into the next compartment where the machinery space is on the centreline but with technical compartments, laundry and electrical, against the shipside. Aft again is the saloon and bar. We thought that it would be better to separate what might be a noisy compartment as far as possible from the voyage crew. Not only were they paying to be onboard but also they were quite likely to be nervous sleepers in a strange environment.

Unfortunately this was bad luck for the paid crew who live right aft. We insulated their accommodation as much as possible on the one hand and encouraged them to fraternise in the bar on the other, and the latter may be the more successful solution. When the aft compartment lift was removed the space on the lower deck level became a tiny out-of-cabin sitting space for the crew. That on the main deck above was taken for an office. Crews on any sail training ship live under considerable pressure and need a certain amount of time off the job in every voyage. On the other hand their customers have a certain right to their company and it is a difficult act to balance in the ship design.

Throughout the development of the ship we were under continual pressure to maximise the number of berths to enhance her earning potential and under another pressure to keep her size within limits both for her practical use and her build costs. We ourselves wanted to get as much eye space as possible both in the deckhouse and below decks as a sovereign specific for the reduction of sea feelings (*mal de mer*). I think we managed that but I cannot say that I am proud of the watch leaders' cabin and I would like to have been able to be more generous with the crew space for her final complement.

There are a number of quite discrete aids about the ship. Raised arrows on the handrails pointing forward for those who cannot see and lighthouse beacons over every watertight door for those who just can. Vibrator alarms are supplied for those who cannot hear ship announcements. The speaking compass is an excellent aid which perhaps should be used by everyone. Over her years of service the Trust have removed a great deal of specialist arrangements for the disabled and that we agree with and are very pleased to see. The wheelchair track remains only as a useful guide about the deck and the hydrocranes for lifting people onto and off the ship went quite early on. Overall we are left with the impression that the regulators are a great deal more at ease with the concept than when we started.

Performance and Balance

When the ship was new she had to be rushed into service to start her earning career and I think it is fair to say that neither we nor Morin Scott were given time for trials. When the word came back from the ship that she carried weather helm we were, of course, very concerned. Proper trials remained impossible and so we started a reporting log so that we could analyse what was happening. It is probably worth going into a little detail over what was actually happening as it illustrates the difference in mental attitudes of those accustomed to different rigs.

It is necessary to point out that the kind of balance that comes with a two-sailed Bermudan yacht is just not possible with square rig. That balance comes from some equivalence between the movements of the centre of pressure of the canvas and the hull as the wind pipes up and the hull moves faster. With seven or eight stacks of sails (i.e. three masts, two sets of intermast staysails and two or three headsails) the movement of the centre of pressure of each sail just cannot meet that of the hull. In a square rigger, therefore, balance at the helm is achieved by the setting and sheeting of sails. For confirmation look at any contemporary painting of a square rigger when they were in their prime showing ships working to windward in strong winds.

We found, after an expensive and thorough analysis, that crew to whom the barque rig was a novelty were trying to set sails as if she were a schooner. It was thought that as the wind increased the sails should be withdrawn towards the centre of the ship. In practice the faster the wind blows the more sail should be concentrated forward. The most notable conclusion was that the forward headsail was not being set. This was the only headsail which was not roller furling and required some crew work at the end of the plank bowsprit. The innermost headsail was not being set because it had to be set part-rolled when the fore course was set and this was not thought to be right. We had made it quite large because the fore course would normally be an early sail to remove when the wind piped up. The situation was further compounded in that the spanker stack was large and beautiful and looked like a schooner mainsail and so it was not only natural to set it but also to sheet it in hard when going to windward.

The spanker stack was the seventh along the length of the vessel. In round terms each vertical stack of sails should converge about five degrees on the next aft to increase the wind driving power. To windward with the outermost headsail set on the edge of lifting, and with each stack slightly converging on the next, by the time you get to the spanker, its boom, hard on the wind, should set some thirty or forty degrees from the centreline. Sheeting it hard in as might seem natural when going to windward just reduces the drive and produces weather helm.

We were very impressed indeed with other aspects of the work of these early crews in a situation which was, to say the least, delicate and important to the

Lord Nelson sailing down channel in a force 9. PHOTO: MAX

OPPOSITE: *Lord Nelson* in the Needles channel returning to her home port of Southampton. PHOTO: MAX

project. We therefore suggested that they should add a little 'topgallant' bowsprit to the end of the main bowsprit, re-arrange the outer headsails and make them all roller furling so that it was easy to set them and take them in. Honour was satisfied, although the influence on ship balance of the tiny extra bowsprit is obviously more tactical than practical.

The Rig

The barque rig is a natural for a training ship of the size of *Lord Nelson*. Intrinsically it provides enough work for the fifty or so souls on board and intrinsically the sails are individually of such a size that they can be set, reefed and handed by a non-horny handed crew. With a certain early emphasis on role reversal we started by planning to give the 'macho' crew roles to the less able. This resulted in an early sail plan with very deep courses on the basis that these would be sheeted by power winches operated by disabled crew. Such deep courses would allow the upper sails to be smaller and therefore more within the anticipated capacity of the crew. Eventually this approach was over-

taken by the addition of another tier of sails, the royals. The slightly deeper than usual courses remain to this day and are handled by the crew without recourse to the winches.

There is something of a myth in the world that the crews of square riggers have to spend perilous time aloft handling the sails and saving the ship at the expense of their fingernails. In fact, crew actually only need to go aloft to loose the sails for setting or to make them up for a harbour stow. The sails are clewed and bunted up from the deck when they have to be taken in. Climbing aloft is a fairly popular aspect of sailing in square riggers and we were concerned that it should not be a divisive aspect of the crew family. It was decided therefore to make the upper square sails roller-furl into their yards. The lower sails were left with the traditional methods of handling but the numbers of crew required aloft for sail handling was reduced to about half and they did not need to climb above the lower top. We planned also to be able to lift wheelchair-bound crew up to the lower tops but our power lifts for this disappeared in the economies of her completion. Probably just as well as they are now hauled aloft by their watch mates, which makes it a much greater feat and pleasure to the whole ship.

The main function of the fore and aft sails on a traditional square rigger was to balance the rig and help in manoeuvring the ship. They also had another valuable function in acting as stabilisers to reduce rolling which adversely affects the all-important flow through the slots of each stack of sails. In *Lord Nelson* we followed the pattern of *Royalist* and made them both bigger and more effective as propulsion sails because we also had motor sailing to consider. All the staysails with one exception were roller-furled. That initial exception was the outermost jib set from the bowsprit end. We did not think that we needed to spend the extra money on this because it would normally be set, we thought, by the professional crew.

The spanker stack has the twin standing gaffs that were a feature of the German ships. These gaffs do not have to be lowered when sail is reduced, the sails being brailed in to gaffs and mast by the crew on deck. The division of the spanker into two sails reduces the handling loads and makes for a convenient and easily worked reef.

It is probably also appropriate to mention the double bowsprit with the mast stays asymmetrically arranged port and starboard to allow the passage of a wheelchair to the outer end. The traditional round section spar bowsprit does not really stand up to any modern logical scrutiny and is ripe for improvement, thanks to modern materials. The arrangement in *Lord Nelson* appears to be very popular with the voyage crews but this may be more to do with the ease of getting out to the end to take photographs. We understand that friends and family of many a wheelchair crew have suffered something of a sea change of attitude when their mariner returns with his or her photographs taken at sea from the bowsprit end.

The Proof of the Pudding ...

Before Chris Rudd and his Jubilee Sailing Trust it is probably fair to say that those people with disabilities who were able to experience the character (and often physical) development of seafaring as a working crew member could be counted on one hand.

In 1999 the JST published the figures for voyagers in *Lord Nelson* since she started work in 1986. The ship had by 1999 taken 15,884 people to sea. Of these 6,431 had physical disabilities and of these 2,627 were wheelchair users. Apart from the benefits to the crew members themselves, kindly carers and indulgent families may often have taken a new and more realistic view of returning crew members from what is perceived to be a macho ship like a square rigger. This additional benefit from the work of the JST has coincided with, and may be responsible for, a considerable and welcome change in attitude to the disabled in general.

The list of the disabilities of those who have crewed in *Lord Nelson* include:

Amputation	295
Blindness	637
Cerebral Palsy	783
Deafness	299
Diabetes	152
Muscular Dystrophy	105
Epilepsy	315
Head Injury	258
Hemiplegia (Stroke)	466
Hydrocephalus	58
Multiple Sclerosis	570
Osteoarthritis	175
Paraplegia	272
Polio	196
Quadriplegia	68
Rheumatoid Arthritis	174
Spina Bifida	469
Spinal Injury	129
Other disabilities	1,459

S.T.S. Young Endeavour

Britain's Bicentennial gift to Australia

1987

Dimensions			
Sparred length		144.00 feet	44.00 metres
Hull length		115.00 feet	35.00 metres
Waterline length		93.00 feet	28.30 metres
Beam		25.60 feet	7.80 metres
Depth		18.60 feet	5.68 metres
Draft		13.10 feet	4.00 metres
Displacement fully laden		239 tonnes	
Full sail area		5,500 square feet	510 square metres
Construction	Steel		
Crew	37		

The Project

When the Australian Bicentennial loomed on the horizon there were many jolly ideas as to how such an event might be most properly celebrated. A reproduction of the 'first fleet' voyage was worked up and with sailing ships converging on Sydney for the occasion, a tall ship event was a natural. We thought that quite the nicest idea was that the British nation should give Australian youth a sail training ship. It is always interesting to know where such absolutely charming thoughts come from. When we were asked to design the ship we met a committee of a considerable proportion of the great and good, all of whom were filled with enthusiasm and hopes. Perhaps it is only fair to note how often one finds Maldwin Drummond, a former chairman of the Sail Training Association, modestly close to the most imaginative projects and we have our suspicions that he may have been the real mainspring.

We were first asked to plan a schooner but discussion quickly turned her into a brigantine. I mention this to explain why the project was often referred to as the bicentennial schooner. She was required to carry twelve male and twelve

OPPOSITE: The brigantine Sail Training Ship *Young Endeavour* – manned by the Royal Australian Navy and crewed by youngsters from all over Australia. PHOTO: IAN MAINSBRIDGE/ *YOUNG ENDEAVOUR* YOUTH SCHEME

female cadets and on her maiden voyage half way around the world these were to be split equally between Australians and British. She was, of course, required to be a good example of her type and tank and wind tunnel testing were in order. Unofficially I was given to understand that unless she won the Bicentennial Hobart to Sydney race Prince Charles might find no takers when he came to hand her over as part of the ceremonies, also that my partners and I would be banished to a durance so vile as to get the ghost of Wilberforce turning in his grave.

Trepidation, that great friend of designers, set in. Parliament had voted the national money for the project, before, as ever, knowing how much she was going to cost. Finance therefore, and such a major date for her hand-over, were immediately two severely imposing features of the project. Arthur Weller, the chairman of the building committee and a man of great maritime experience, was thoroughly aware of the pitfalls in building a small vessel on one side of the globe for delivery on the other. All in all it was a very nervous time.

The ship had to be special. Not only did she have to have square rig performance but she had to have some element of appearance that would note to all those that saw her that she was Britain's gift and all this had to be in a packet which would be acceptable to old and new seamen alike. Buckingham Palace had authorised that she could be painted *Britannia* blue – a very signal honour which really got us started. The ship, we thought, must be both modern in appearance and have some elements of tradition. The earlier Victorian Royal yachts seemed to give us some clues and you may see some reflection of them in the long straight sheer, slightly exaggerated bow and short full stern.

And so to work. We tank tested a model at the Wolfson Unit in Southampton and followed it by wind tunnel testing of a model of the rig. Olin Stephens used to say that he tank tested to check that some drawing board development had not actually ruined anything else and we rather have the same attitude. We needed the tank testing for this reassurance for the project and were pleased to see that she seemed to be reasonably dry on deck when put to work amongst sample wave patterns. We were also pleased to see that the hull developed more side force than any other square rigger we had tested. The side force developed by a hull is a necessary ingredient in the windward ability of the ship at sea.

Wind tunnel testing is, in square rig, more difficult to assess because of the multiples of potential sail settings. We had already decided to get the yards braced slightly further than we had managed before, in fact to twenty-seven to twenty-eight degrees. In the tunnel we developed the width of the square yards and experimented with a quadrilateral staysail, which we hoped might be something of a secret weapon. These quads were an everyday sail for centuries before the economies came in at the end of the nineteenth century. Then they disappeared so completely, presumably because they required a larger crew, that many a shellback has told us that they were never used. However, this one seemed to give us a bit of help when hard on the wind and we thought that at the very least it would be education for the trainees.

The yacht division of Brooke Marine at Lowestoft were chosen to build the ship and we were very pleased with this both because of their admirable steel-work and large building sheds. They had also recently built a warship for the Australian Navy which gave them, we thought, some better insight into any 'down under' aspects. Our confidence faltered a moment or two when Brooke Marine got into financial problems about half way through the work. Fortunately they re-emerged as Brooke Yachts who went on to finish the ship in fine style. She was, in fact, built in a thoroughly modern manner in sections which could be part fitted out before being assembled into a ship. Before she was launched her appointed Captain, Chris Blake, made a very solemn and complete inspection of the ship and every detail of her and the standards of work to emerge down the gangway again with only three words *'I'll buy her'*.

Launching was another day for nerves, not because of any naval architectural concern but because the launching crane got a riding turn and while this was being cleared with wedges and hammers the tide started away on what was likely the last possible adequate stand of tide for some days. However, she was safely launched by the Duchess of Kent and towed round to her fitting out basin to be rigged. Some weeks later Chris took her to sea for her first trials off Lowestoft with her Australian and British crew, both groups having survived a Royal Marine type selection programme. Trials turned into acceptance trials but what made my day was that Chris showed his confidence in the ship and took her back into Lowestoft harbour and into the lock under sail with everything set.

The wheels then rolled along to get her on her way, this included a great deal of ceremonial although we did get some more sailing in her in the Solent. Finally she left Cowes with guns firing, huzzas ringing out and families waving farewell to offspring bound half way around the world. She dipped her ensign to *S.T.S. Lord Nelson*, and set off to the westward, mirroring the painting Charles Munro had made of the ship some months before. Perhaps it is not quite fair to recount this, but when we took the Yarmouth to Lymington ferry back home, hoping to see her, there she was, hove-to and pointing back towards the east while she got over a little 'finger trouble', as Chris described it. We confess to provoking the Lymington ferry Captain into calling him up on the radio and pointing out that Australia was actually in the other direction. Chris Blake had a more than suitable revenge a couple of months later. I had a telephone call from him from the ship in the Southern Ocean. My immediate reaction was: *'The masts must still be in her if he can make the call'* and all sorts of maritime disasters flashed in front of my eyes as he knew they would. Chris just said, *'We have been doing fourteen knots all night and thought you ought to know about it'* and with that he rang off.

When Rosemary and I arrived in Sydney for the Bicentennial we had had little news of the race from Hobart and so, despite it being late at night, we diverted our taxi to the docks to see if any ships had arrived, but there was none. In our hotel room we turned on the TV and there was a shot of *Young Endeavour* coming up the harbour. First thing next morning we went to see her in what was, to us, a particularly pleasingly empty dock. Chris Blake had done his stuff and the hand-over could go ahead on the steps of the Opera House with confidence.

It was a marvellous occasion. One Australian newspaper, suggesting what the newspaper headlines might have been some two hundred years earlier when the first fleet arrived, came up with *'We have got to watch these boat people'*.

The Lines

In the high profile climate prevailing in this project, this was obviously a vessel which had to be at least a bit notable in appearance and in performance. We were in fact faced with something of a challenge. With *Royalist*, *Varuna* and *Lord Nelson* behind us it seemed that it would be rather perverse to ignore them and to strike off in any different direction. The same factors prevailed. This was to be a sailing ship which would not carry cargo, should be a stable and dry platform for her cadets and manoeuvre easily so as not to break their hearts. Every pointer directed us to develop what we had. Time, as ever, was short but we were able to check our hull form in the Wolfson test tank.

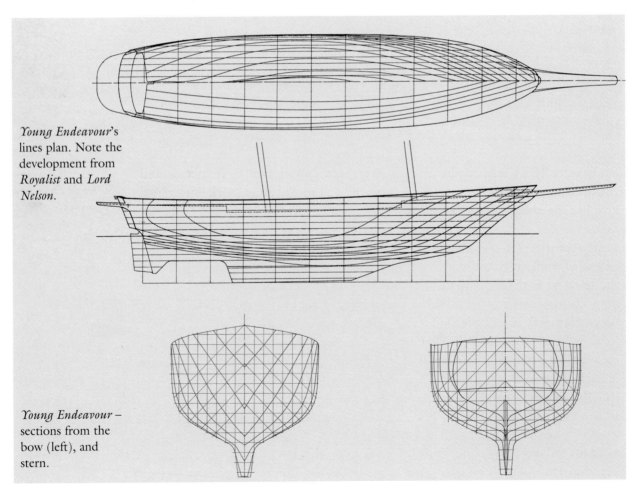

Young Endeavour's lines plan. Note the development from *Royalist* and *Lord Nelson*.

Young Endeavour – sections from the bow (left), and stern.

Essentially we shaped the aft end after *Lord Nelson* with an immersed and cut-off transom. This gives the long, low and well spread aft buttock lines which give her the ability to sail fast in strong winds at some small expense of light air performance. They also help to give good directional stability which makes for easier steering by the cadets. Above the water we gave her, like *Lord Nelson*, an extended hull over the transom. This has several virtues of which perhaps the greatest is that it reduces the impact of following seas by ironing out the immersion of the hull buoyancy. It also protects the air ventilated rudder and is very cost effective in accommodation space for building costs.

The below water profile is that of the conventional sailing ship of history with an added ballast keel and deep rudder and skeg. The function of the added keel is interesting. It is there initially as part of the stability package and to help control the rate of rolling. It is there also to act as a sailing keel for its value for windward work. Not so often appreciated perhaps is that it helps to stabilise the variations of the hull pressures with different speeds. This shows up in a reduced need for sail work to keep the helm in balance. For *Young Endeavour* we gave the keel perhaps a little more depth than we might have done for European waters.

About half the crew of *Young Endeavour* on her forecastle head. PHOTO: IAN MAINSBRIDGE/ *YOUNG ENDEAVOUR* YOUTH SCHEME

She has a good chicken breast forefoot which softens the hull motion when moving fast in a seaway while retaining the asymmetry between bow and stern which prevents the build up of rhythmical pitching in a seaway. The deep rudder reduces the steering loads and the profile between keel and rudder skeg is reputed to cause vortices which are supposed to enhance the rudder effect if the ship should assume a heavy angle of heel.

With our best done below water we then gave her a well raked clipper stem. Apart from lightening the appearance of a good full hull and shortening the bowsprit it makes an excellent lead into a well flared bow which helps to keep the decks dry when sailing fast in a seaway. You can see that wherever the word 'fast' appeared on one side or other of the consideration we slipped in that direction. We had, with the *Britannia* blue hull and dark red boot-top, an essentially dark skinned vessel. Also we had the brigantine rig to set it off. Both of these were at their peak of appearance in the Victorian yachts.

Walk Through

There were several main components to the accommodation planning of *Young Endeavour*. First, perhaps, that she was to be a warm weather ship – at least to our North Sea standards. This infers that a considerable part of the life of the ship will be on deck and therefore it should be big, open and spacious. Second was that she was to be planned for embarking boys and girls in equal numbers. For this it means that sleeping and washing arrangements should be able to be split down the middle and that both halves should be equal and opposite. To a degree this exact equality was a bit counter-productive in that we could not slip in the slightly larger washroom and lockerage that we usually try to get in for the feminine half. We believe that this is a practical and not a sexist attitude. At least we get told about this with some frequency.

The third component was the realisation that people were expecting much more from sail training than the simple pleasures of getting exhausted, soaked and frightened with their mates. A suitable ship must have the ability for her crew to participate in rather more upmarket activities. I think that it was Maldwin Drummond who insisted that she be fitted out for oceanography and between us we also planned for room to carry boats for watersports and arranged space for lectures and so on. The overall principle was that she should be flexible in her arrangement to cater for the changing role the sail training ship might experience in her planned fifty-year life.

The oceanography requirement confirmed the value of the stern platform at one end and the dolphin bowsprit at the other, for these were both areas where scientists could stand to monitor both wildlife and their scientific kit. The dolphin plank bowsprit seems to us to be the logical modern form for sail training ships as it has become in cruising yachts, and indeed motor cruisers. Our only regret is that we did not at the same time make provision for a bowsprit net as

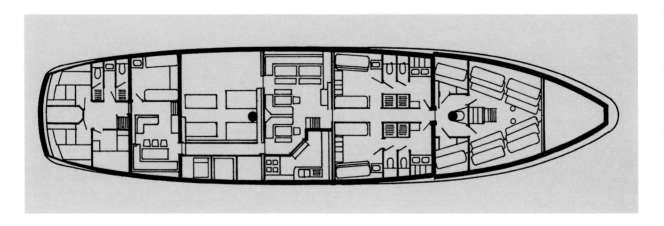

well. It is not a necessity with our walk-out bowsprit but we half regret not fitting one, unnecessary or not, for the sheer pleasure it gives to all who dream in it as they are suspended over the sparkling ocean.

The only deckhouse is aft of the mainmast and this is the charthouse which also includes a technical bench for the scientists. At the aft end there is a single companion down to the wardroom and twin short companions up to the bridge (for naval personnel) or cockpit (for a yachtsman). The steering and instruments are all here and it is covered in a pipe framework. This has a dual role. Essentially it provides a crash bar to protect the cockpit team should, for instance, the spanker boom ever get out of control. For everyday use it is an awning frame. At the aft end of the cockpit there is another companion to the officers' quarters. There are three proper cabins for the main afterguard. Two are right aft and to starboard is the cabin at the foot of the companion for the Captain. On the other side of the lobby is a double washroom. This is all aft of the after watertight bulkhead. Ahead of it is the wardroom to starboard and a general accommodation cabin for junior officers to port. In truth, this is a compartment of pipe cots and standard lockers exactly matching the accommodation for the trainees forward. The only concession to the afterguard status is that it has its own washbasin and immediate access to the wardroom.

To one side of the next compartment forward, which contains the machinery, is an alley with the laundry, cold room and main galley store. The galley is immediately forward again so the cook has only a short step to his stores. The galley is on the starboard side of the main messdeck for the good reason that a sailing ship is usually hove-to, in bad weather, on the starboard tack which gives her theoretical right of way over any other ships around. On the starboard tack this galley will therefore be 'up' and any detritus from capsized plates and cadets will tend to slip away from it, which may be thought to be more hygienic.

Ahead of this is the main cadet accommodation of two six-berth compartments, washrooms, and a twelve-berth forecastle which may, if required, be split down the middle. Also in this space is a good sized lobby with cabins port and starboard. These were planned for the visiting scientists or other experts but may also be used for watch leaders.

The below deck arrangement of *Young Endeavour*, with berths for twelve male cadets forward and twelve female cadets amidships. The small cabins in between are for watch leaders or scientists.

A visual of *S.T.S. Young Endeavour* painted by Arthur Saluz before she was built. She is flying the red ensign as this is, of course, before she was handed over to Australia.

Young Endeavour is plentifully equipped with watertight bulkheads and, in fact, meets the two-compartment standard of flotation which means that she should stay afloat with any two compartments flooded. A one-compartment standard is required for sail training ships but we think that a two-compartment standard should be planned if at all possible. Bulkhead doors have to be left open for the normal access of a sailing ship crew about the interior of the ship. They are, of course, closed in any situation where peril might be perceived ahead, such as crossing shipping lanes, entering harbour or in fog. However, it would be too easy for a single door to be left unclipped in any sudden emergency. We are also concerned that collision with rocks or large fast ferries might rip the skin right across any single bulkhead. Note also that with the exception of a single bulkhead all the watertight doors are on the centreline, which materially delays the spillage from one compartment to another should she be heavily heeled if the skin is pierced. Such disasters are not pleasant to contemplate on the drawing board or anywhere else but it has to be done.

Performance

Charles Munro's painting of *S.T.S. Young Endeavour* leaving for Australia. He has shown her just outside the Isle of Wight with *Royalist* in the distance.

We always try to impose on the captains of new vessels a performance-reporting log. This really only asks them that when the ship is sailing along in something of a steady state they, or the Officer of the Watch, should just note down all the instrument readings. Over a period of time this can build up into a complete picture of what the ship has actually achieved. We take the best performances and plot them out, where they serve both for our office education and as objectives for the crew on subsequent voyages. This is really a good old-fashioned approach for want of an appropriate black box which would report everything automatically. Next ship, we always say, we will get the theoretical performance on the ship's computer and the reporting black box on the satellite. It is everyday technology but not yet for us it would seem.

However, *Young Endeavour* kept a close log on her performance on her delivery voyages up to hand-over and her Captain, Chris Blake, sent us the

Young Endeavour – this polar diagram shows the performance over a wide range of sailing, reported on her voyage to Australia. Note that her best performance to windward is about fifty-five degrees off the true wind.

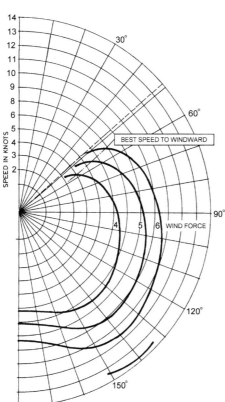

figures which are shown in polar diagram form. This shows the hull speeds achieved right around the compass for the normal range of wind speeds. The further up the graph the curves go indicates the best speed to windward and the further down they go is the best speed when running. It can be seen that she makes her best footing to windward with the wind at some fifty-five degrees and, in the other direction, she makes the best progress with the wind some twenty degrees on the quarter, not with the wind dead aft.

It may be interesting to see how critical is the angle of the ship to windward. Luff her up just a few degrees and she will lose speed rapidly and with hull speed a major factor in reducing leeway it can be seen that getting a square rigger to windward requires much more accurate helmsmanship than for a modern yacht. The Captain of a clipper ship beating out of the English Channel or the China Sea would often keep on deck for the whole of the windward leg.

Sail Plan

The original concept was for a vessel rigged as a schooner to follow the great traditions set for sail training by the two famous British schooners *Sir Winston Churchill* and *Malcolm Miller*. Since the 1960s, when they were designed, the benefits of square rig for sail training have become accepted and the logical step forward from a schooner took us to the brigantine. Essentially this is a vessel with a conventional square rig on the foremast and a conventional schooner rig on the main. Fortunately the rig has settled down to the label of brigantine for at one stage in the last century it might have been identified as a 'hermaphrodite brig'. Should any antique purists continue to take that line we can rather smugly point out that *Young Endeavour* was, in fact and from the very beginning, specifically planned for use by both sexes.

Brigantines would seem to have two origins for their rig. The sharp cutters used by Navies and Customs in the nineteenth century were sometimes equipped with a full set of squaresails in addition to their normal cutter rig to increase their potential for the downwind chase. In this guise they were called cutter-brigs and it is easy to see that their next step forward would be to lengthen the ship and fit another and separate mast for the squaresails. It is possible to see a link between these sharp-bowed vessels with squaresails all the way to the development of the great clipper ships. The other origin is not quite as attractive but relates to the rises in seamen's wages which led ship owners to look for some method of reducing crew numbers. Converting a stack of squaresails to fore and aft allowed a considerable reduction in crew at the expense of some light weather performance. It is tempting to put two other factors to the development of the rig. First, that steam tugs were available to pluck ships in and out of harbour in light airs and therefore light weather performance was no longer such a criterion. Second, that the brigantine was not classed as a square rigged vessel for the Merchant Shipping Acts and therefore the masters did not require a square rig ticket.

With our previous experience of square rig we did not start with the often-believed notion that it was no use to windward. We were able to plan from the beginning that the whole rig would function throughout the range of performance rather than to allocate the fore and aft rig to windward work and the square rig to downwind duties. We planned that the yards would swing round to twenty-eight degrees from the centreline and were very careful with the design of the slots. The masts were given a heavy rake. This was not to add lift to the squaresails of the forebody but to improve the way the fore and aft sails hung off the mainmast. Raked masts promote chafe in the squaresails but we had extended the trusses to achieve our bracing angles and this helped. Incidentally, square sails, properly kited and sheeted to enhance the slots between them, do all the lifting the bow could ask for.

Slightly against the best traditions for brigantines we gave her a standing rather than a lowering gaff. The latter can be a killer if it gets loose and is definitely not on for a cadet ship of this size. The headsails follow, if anything, the cutter tradition and the main interest of all brigantines is what sails are hung up between the masts. We opted for the simplicity of two roller-furling staysails but we added a large quadrilateral for what we call a 'Sunday sail'. That is, a sail specifically planned for the dictionary definition of yachting – that is, for pleasure or for racing. We put the whole lot into the Wolfson wind tunnel in Southampton and we found to our satisfaction that the big quadrilateral staysail actually improved her performance when hard on the wind.

There remains a certain regret that we did not fully pursue the benefits of the quadrilateral. It was after all a traditional sail used with square rig for many years. However, it was rarely set close coupled to the foremast as we, brought up on the Bermudan rig, had put it but set off the mast with a lacing by as much as a metre. There remains a small feeling that this would have extended its range of valuable drive from simply hard on the wind.

K.L.D. Tunas Samudera

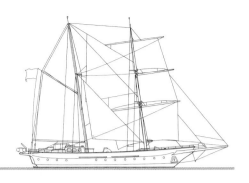

Young Endeavour's Malaysian sister ship

1989

Dimensions

Sparred length	144.00 feet	44.00 metres
Hull length	115.00 feet	35.00 metres
Waterline length	93.00 feet	28.30 metres
Beam	25.60 feet	7.80 metres
Depth	18.60 feet	5.68 metres
Draft	13.10 feet	4.00 metres
Displacement fully laden	239 tonnes	
Full sail area	5,500 square feet	510 square metres
Construction	Steel	
Crew	37	

OPPOSITE: *K.L.D. Tunas Samudera* was handed over to the Royal Malaysian Navy by H.M. the Queen Elizabeth II and H.M. the King of Malaysia, Sultan Azlan Shah, in a joint ceremony at Lumut Naval Base, Malaysia, in August 1989. PHOTO: ROSEMARY MUDIE

K.L.D. (Royal Malaysian Navy Ship) *Tunas Samudera* is operated by the Malaysian Navy for Malaysian youngsters. VISUAL BY ARTHUR SALUZ

151

The official hand-over of *Tunas Samudera* to the Malaysian Navy at their Lamut Naval Base was one of those occasions which seems unbelievable in recollection. There we were, with various VIPs, in a sun-shelter marquee on the jetty facing our ship. The Royal yacht *Britannia* then hove in view and quietly moored to the other side of the jetty with her warps coming ashore exactly as the clocks struck the exact hour of her scheduled arrival. The Queen and Prince Philip disembarked to be greeted by the King of Malaysia and the other Kings of the Federation and by the Admirals. They all mustered in the marquee for the dedication ceremonies and in her speech the Queen said that the presentation of a sail training ship was a most appropriate symbol of the heritage shared by the peoples of Britain and Malaysia. Her Majesty continued by saying:

> 'Naval and commercial ships may no longer use sails for their propulsion, but the sea and the elements have not changed. Storms, tides, darkness and fog still provide a challenge to the skills and nerve of the professional seaman.

> 'There is no better way of gaining an understanding of the arts of seaman-ship and navigation than the experience of managing a ship under sail. Training under sail is a challenging adventure. It demands discipline, skill and knowledge and it teaches the value of teamwork and honest commit-ment for the sake of everyone on board. There is no room for selfishness when the lives of all on board are at stake.'

Our Royals, their Royals and all the top brass then took the red carpet path to board and inspect *Tunas Samudera,* who was as clean and polished and as smart as every sail training ship should be. Satisfaction apparent, they regained the jetty, and the Royal Marine band from *Britannia* marched and played. The Queen and Prince Philip re-embarked and *Britannia* unmoored, again to the minute and, looking as magnificent as ever, slowly sailed away into the Malaysian sunshine. I do not want to beat an old drum but it was a fine example of the value of Royalty in a Royal yacht in making a ceremony magical and, with it, goodwill for all us Brits and all we do.

Tunas Samudera is a sister ship to *Young Endeavour* with only the most modest changes. To reduce her build period she was built with full steel under-decks in place of the open structure we prefer. The slight extra weight this involved required a very small addition of ballast to give her the same stability pattern as *Young Endeavour.* So that they could race on level terms we added a few extra square feet of sail but that was all.

Tunas Samudera was ordered not long after a visit to Malaysia by Prime Minister Thatcher and we suspect, without proof of course, that she understood the need for nations to have sail training ships. The ship had to be built in quick time by Brooke Yachts, the same builders as for *Young Endeavour,* and her masts were stepped and her spars fitted before she was embarked onboard a heavy-lift

ship and taken to Singapore for further fit-out before making her way to Malaysia and her hand-over. She was accompanied on the voyage by her boatswain, Rod Lance, who spent the voyage rigging her. From his vantage up *Tunas Samudera*'s masts he discovered that he could look straight into the bridge of the ship and interpret various hospitable gestures when the sun rose over the yard arms. We have often wondered if this long voyage was a record for a singlehanded crew on a 35 metre brigantine.

Sadly *Tunas Samudera* and *Young Endeavour* have only raced together once, at Sail Indonesia '95 and the result was inconclusive. A pity, the two of them driving towards a camera would have made a rather pleasing picture.

K.L.D. Tunas Samudera (Offspring of the Ocean) BY KIND PERMISSION OF THE MALAYSIAN MINISTRY OF DEFENCE

153

I.N.S. Tarangini

Lord Nelson's Indian Navy sister ship

1997

Dimensions			
Sparred length		177.00 feet	54.00 metres
Hull length		140.00 feet	42.80 metres
Beam		28.00 feet	8.50 metres
Draft		13.00 feet	4.00 metres
Sail area		12,241 square feet	1,035 square metres
Construction	Steel		
Crew	60		

The Project

O ver a period of some years we had what we thought were rather unofficial enquiries from the Indian Navy. These were about a sail training ship to take officer cadets to sea for sail training experience. We prepared a couple of sets of plans along the way – for forty-one metre and for fifty metre barques. For 1988 the Indian Navy borrowed *Varuna* to attend the Australian Bicentennial celebrations in Sydney and clearly remained interested in the value of sail training for their officer cadets. So when in due course I was summoned to Delhi, knowing that the stringencies of the Indian economy might scupper anything too lavish, I took with me a proposition based on the *Young Endeavours*. They were well proven vessels but we had thought that the twenty-four cadet complement might not be economic for everyone. We had therefore, on paper, lengthened her by a cot length. In practice this would translate in berths for another eight or twelve. The additional length also allowed us to rig her as a barque which gave better employment for the extra numbers.

My presentation to the Navy was largely based on Max's photographs of sail training ships and sail training occasions. *Lord Nelson* of course was well represented and it may have been his pictures of her that swung the committee towards a *Lord Nelson*. She did look particularly well on the screen. Even so, it was the start of a high level technical discussion on every aspect of the ship. What they would require was not a sister ship but one based on a proven hull and rig, wrapped around their own very detailed staff requirements. Discussion

OPPOSITE: The Indian Navy sail training ship *I.N.S. Tarangini* off Visakhapatnam in the Bay of Bengal.
PHOTO: MAX

on every aspect continued in London and with visits to *Lord Nelson* herself so that the Indian Navy representatives and potential builders could become acclimatised to the tasks ahead. On one visit to the ship in Plymouth the delegation made such a close examination of every nook and cranny in the hull that I thought that they would wish to examine every detail aloft. It was blowing hard and raining at the time and no-one was more relieved than I was when it turned out that the last train back to London made such an inspection, regretfully, impossible.

Compared with *Lord Nelson* the new ship has a completely different layout both below and above decks. We took the opportunity to recess the anchors whose big flat bottoms sticking out of the bow of *Lord Nelson* were something of an economy measure. We did not need the big plank bowsprit for wheelchairs and replaced it with a conventional pole which with bowsprit netting is better enjoyed by fully able cadets. We also retained the stern platform sticking out past the transom. Although never used in *Lord Nelson* for its intended purpose (disabled access to boats) it has been an unexpectedly popular feature over several ships. It seems to be good for the storage of petrol cans, warps and even bicycles and also for sunbathing and fishing when the weather is set fair.

Eventually the Specification was initialled on every one of its hundred and twenty-six closely discussed and agreed pages. A contract for the design work was prepared for signing with our teaming partners, Three Quays Marine Services. We have an easy relationship with this eminent group and divide design work between us as may be most convenient. The rough line of division is that they are engineering and systems while we are hulls, layouts and sail power. At the same time we were informed that the Indian Navy had allocated the building work to the Indian government builders, Goa Shipyard Ltd. They had also allocated them to us as our clients. It was an unusual arrangement. The Indian Navy appeared to have retired over the horizon while keeping full control over the builders to whom this was a quite new kind of vessel. Incidentally the last sailing ship built in Goa was, we think, a wooden wall.

We found the yard to be a very well-equipped steel-building establishment with all the latest kit, fine sheds and good slips. We also found an excellent technical staff, anxious to learn, and with whom we soon had a very good relationship. Over the build period two important facets of the work emerged. We suspect that practically everyone involved must have thought that a little sailing ship must be streets easier to build than the complex warships which were their normal daily fare. This, we might note, is a curiously common attitude amongst modern shipbuilders. The other facet, however, surprised us greatly. So modern was the yard that they really had little acquaintance with wood. We had believed the west coast of India was a world heritage site for the crafts and craftsmen of wood construction. In other projects we had seen west coast Indian craftsmen imported to other countries to build ships in wood. It was, for us, a cultural shock to realise that even the fitting of wooden decks would be an ongoing source of discussion.

An Arthur Saluz visual of *I.N.S.* (Indian Navy Ship) *Tarangini.*

She took rather longer to build than planned because she had to be completed outdoors because of warship pressures on the building sheds. Also, it might be noted that there were hold-ups and delays from some of the non-sailing military specialists. Very properly they wanted to optimise their specialities and proposed and planned away beyond the agreed Specification without realising the consequences for a sailing ship. It is not the first time that we have been presented with a scheme for aerials which mean that not a single sail can be set.

The inconvenient intrusions of the monsoon made for further delays but eventually she was completed. Captain Homi Motivala set about coming to terms with his new barque. He came from racing Olympic dinghies and had a very welcome analytical approach to optimising her sailing. Later he also embarked Frank Scott and they and the ship's officers sailed *Tarangini* thousands of miles with a rather scratch crew (including a proportion of cooks and stewards) before the officer cadet crew joined for their training. When we went for trials we were delighted and impressed with this first crew who would box-haul her for fun and took pride in their sail setting, tacking and gybing.

Walk Through

Tarangini is a sail training ship which will normally operate in the warmer climes of India although it is hoped that she will represent her country in due course in the great gatherings of ships. On deck she has three smallish deckhouses leaving

the nice clear open decks which give space, access and communication which are valuable for the training and teamwork of sailing ships. The forward deckhouse is mostly galley and can serve meals directly to the crew on deck or, by means of a small food lift, to the main messdeck under. This deckhouse also includes the main companion access to the messdeck below and a small private mess for the petty officers. This latter also serving as a check-in for cadets joining ship.

The next deckhouse aft is a large charthouse with four chart tables – that is one for the real navigator and one for each cadet watch. At the fore end there is a companion ladder to the accommodation under so that internal access can be maintained throughout the ship in bad weather. At the aft end there are two companions to what we have called the cockpit (although it is raised clear of the deck) and the crew call the bridge. This is the command and steering position and includes the mizzenmast and its pinrail. Aft of that is the third deckhouse with its main companion to the wardroom and aft accommodation. It includes

I.N.S. Tarangini (She who rides the waves) PHOTO: MAX

OPPOSITE: The hull of *I.N.S. Tarangini* building in Goa Shipyard Ltd. PHOTO: MAX

159

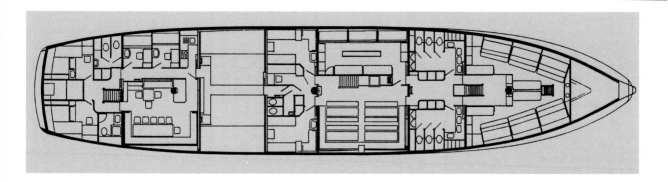

Tarangini's arrangement below decks. The cadets sleep forward, the officers aft, and the petty officers and seamen amidships.

the ship's office and a small communications room. This latter allows the Commanding Officer privacy in his discussions with, for instance, headquarters.

This 'best' companion is specially considered. On the one hand it is the fast route up for the Captain and officers to the bridge and on the other it is the gracious route down for important visitors to the wardroom. It actually leads to a lobby with cabins for the Captain and the Chief Officer to starboard and port. Between these is the steering compartment which we insulate to some extent with wardrobes and more formal insulation. I must confess, however, that we really rather like the idea of the cadets on the helm knowing that the top brass onboard are going to be aware of every movement of the steering wheel. It helps to teach them to 'steer small' and to stop waving the ship all over the ocean.

The wardroom is separated from the rest of the officer accommodation by a passage with a pantry at the fore end. It would not be appropriate for all the officers' meals to be prepared in the deck galley and be marched aft to their table.

The next bit of ship is the machinery space with a pair of large Kirloscar Cummins main engines and a pair of Kirloscar Cummins generators, each, by non-naval standards, twice the usual size. A small triumph for our engineering designers is that when we were onboard the engine room was the coolest part of the ship with crew slipping in for a snooze in their watch below. A walkway through the engine room opens forward into a small area for the professional crew. This has separate cabins for the seamen and the petty officers, their own washroom, and the ship's sickbay.

From there to the collision bulkhead she is rather tightly packed with cadets. There are three fifteen-berth compartments and the dining and instruction mess deck. We did not really plan them to be so well packed but in place of our normal folding cots we found that the ship was issued with standard military units of impressive stature. In addition there are two quite sizeable washrooms giving about a one to eight ratio of facilities to cadets.

There are many felicities in the bringing into service of a new ship. Two I would like to mention. First that the officers had redesigned the wardroom layout to make it less formal – a feature often found in a happy ship. Second was that the Captain was able to get up on the deckhouse tops from the cockpit (bridge) and with the two walkways could see and directly supervise every aspect of the work about the decks.

The Cadland Ship

A great sailing ship for the nation

Dimensions		
Sparred length	432.00 feet	131.50 metres
Hull length	369.00 feet	112.50 metres
Hull beam	47.50 feet	14.50 metres
Draft	23.00 feet	7.00 metres
Sail area	36,000 square feet	3,400 square metres
Displacement	3,500 tons	
Construction	Steel	
Crew	60	
Voyage crew	180	

The Project

The last vessel in this run through history was one into which we all put a great deal of work, planning – and dreams. When it was announced that the Royal Yacht *Britannia* was to be decommissioned a number of us who had seen what that vessel had done for Britain thought it inconceivable that she should not have a successor. *Britannia* herself is, I think, a unique vessel. She was designed by shipbuilders, not yacht builders, and their ideas as to what a yacht should look like were both slightly unusual and gloriously successful. Wherever *Britannia* went she had a presence which lifted the ships and docks and harbours around her onto a different and more eminent plane. The *Britannia* effect also touched her crew and their seamanship and shiphandling were a pleasure to behold. You can see that we thought that the country would be the lesser without her.

Times and Britain had changed. A dear old *Britannia* reflecting tradition was acceptable, a direct replacement would not be. For one thing there would seem to be some competition between monarchs, tycoons and other wealthy people to build ever bigger and more impressive motor yachts. A new *Britannia*, inevitably reflecting British standing in the world, could not, we thought, ever compete in size. Even if we built the biggest yacht today she could be outclassed tomorrow. We had a healthy dislike of seeing our monarch in her yacht being parked with the smaller vessels.

In any case we were all involved, one way or another, with sail training. We knew of the great interest our Royal family took in sail training and how often they attended events and how many sail training organisations they supported. We also knew and regretted that Britain was one of the few major maritime nations which did not have a major sail training ship seen as a nationally owned vessel. The two aspects clicked naturally together and we set forth to suggest that any replacement for *Britannia* should take the form of a sail training ship. The size problem of the motor yacht does not affect sailing ships in the same way. There would seem to be a natural maximum effective size for wind power due, we think, to the fact that the winds of heaven blow at the same speed for all. Any ship larger than the one we were proposing would be unlikely to perform as well under sail.

We planned a representative ship, sourced the money to build her, and did our business plans to show that she could more than earn her keep. We gave her enough back-up engine power to guarantee tight schedule keeping and planned her to be a zero emission ship. We pointed out that sail training events were of themselves the greatest spectator sports all over the world and that the arrival in port of a large sailing ship was a thoroughly notable occasion, Royal or not. We said that a sail training ship is the ultimate non-threatening national presence.

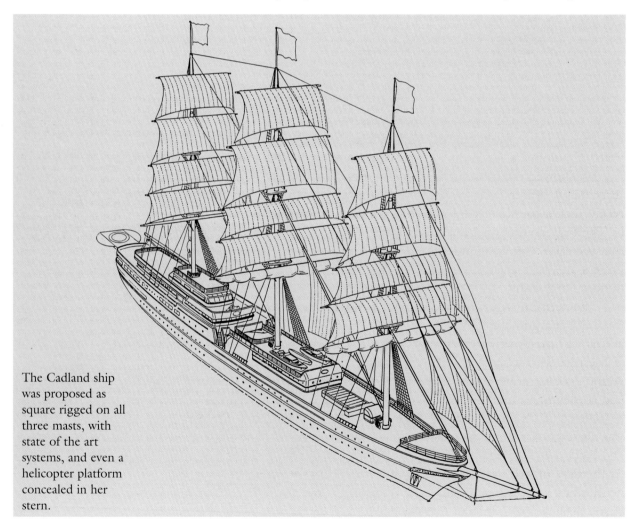

The Cadland ship was proposed as square rigged on all three masts, with state of the art systems, and even a helicopter platform concealed in her stern.

We quoted diplomats as saying that the presence of a large sail training ship with her complement of well behaved and handsome young people was worth seven years of diplomacy.

We showed the plans and a model to politicians, civil servants, naval architects, naval officers, and also on television and at exhibitions. All in all we received an astonishing degree of support countrywide and even internationally. The only doubts we heard came from the Royal Navy who were concerned that the care of their monarch at sea would move from the two hundred or so professional seamen of *Britannia* to the sixty or so permanent crew and one hundred and eighty cadets of our ship.

The decision was, after all, not to have any replacement for *Britannia*. The force of our arguments remain. With the implications of a full Royal palace afloat at least reduced, perhaps we can dream on to a ship which will combine national prestige with a sea experience and training role for an extended range of young people, to give them a career enhancer combined with the unforgettable and challenging experience of crewing a seagoing national ambassador.

The name *Cadland* for the project was our code name before the proposition was made public. It refers to the house of our Chairman, Maldwin Drummond.

At the time of writing a Cadland type project is just beginning to feel the most gentle, but noticeably fair, zephyrs of national opinion carrying her forward. Hope springs...

An Arthur Saluz visual of 'the Cadland ship', proposed as a Royal sail training ship following the decommissioning of the Royal Yacht *Britannia*.

EPILOGUE

A book like this with its drive through history ought to arrive at some conclusions. Furthermore it would seem customary for these conclusions to include some visionary views of the future of its subject.

The conclusions I have come to, after what might be politely described as many years of study, is that it is too easy to get over-intense. I walk around the various gatherings of sailing vessels, large and small, and find few that are not open to criticism on some point or other. I can agonise over the layout of the rig, the safety of getting about the decks or the logic of the hull form. I find that I worry about some rudder stocks and some anchors and some liferafts. I look to see if the navigation lights can actually be seen from dead ahead and groan to myself if the brasswork is not polished and the varnishwork not bright. In short I am a misery to myself on these occasions and probably to everyone else as well.

I have to remind myself that these very same vessels have probably been at sea doing their job for years, that generations have sailed them in safety and pleasure. I need to remind myself also that modern sailing craft have unrivalled statistics for safety and reliability and that all round the world increasing numbers of people are taking to them for pleasure. This need to remind myself is compounded when I see sailing vessels, from small yachts to great square riggers, at sea. Their beauty and confidence is quite breathtaking and quite obliterates my petty harbour concerns. Under sail myself I find little trace of these concerns.

A conclusion, therefore, must be to acknowledge that it is not too difficult to arrive at a competent sailing vessel which will do all that is asked of it. The wind in a sail is a forgiving power unit that will drive almost anything. It needs a very unusual hull form not to develop some windward lift when forward drive and sideways drift combine into what we now call an angle of attack. Resins and weldings have given us competent hull envelopes to keep us and our household goods warm and dry. Domestic power and plumbing are probably as big a factor in choice of a new boat as any basic concerns about details of its assembly or

performance. In short we may be rather pleased with ourselves in any placing in a pantheon of sailing history.

And yet, and yet, there is so much more we could be doing. There may be so much that our ancestors could have told us. There may be so much of what we do now that will amaze future generations. Much of it may be contained in the riddle of why modern yachts heel over despite ballast keels and fleshy hedges sitting low around the weather edge of the deck while keel-less modern wind-surfers stand up tall and, more often than not, heel to windward.

So my first visionary view of the future lies in a return to historical standards of heel when under sail allied with a re-appreciation of our principal heeling agent – the sport-oriented and expensive Bermudan rig. Next must come a decline in visible rigging in the larger ships. We only have the multiples of shrouds and standing rigging because that was necessary for the materials of yesteryear. Again, we only have so much visible running rigging these days, whistling in the wind, because it was impossible to put any of it inside wooden spars. The same reason used to make it necessary to manually harbour-stow our sails and most of us still do it.

When it comes to hull construction, however, I can prophesy with safety. Small sailing vessels now lead the way and the larger ones must catch up. It was Sir John Thornycroft who said that all worthwhile developments came from small craft. He spoilt the remark a bit in our eyes by adding that they were, of course, so much cheaper than large craft.

The way we build in steel these days would have Henry Ford in a lather. We still build in steel as if it was a novel alternative to wood whose construction style we should follow. We still can see how provision is made to take the strains of long dead caulkers pounding ghostly wooden plank seams. We build intricate structures that are long on labour costs and short on ship life. We still build a hull and then fit it out with piping and ducting although one could note that there are some small improvements to be seen here. We still indulge in system racing where the first plumber in gets the straight and easy pipe runs. We still carry the furnishing into our hulls and we still use paint brushes and sprays. We still use propellers and rudders, and on and on. The list is endless and full of promise. Things may be improving but my own discipline, naval architecture, has a lot to do.

GLOSSARY

A glossary of some of the terms in the context in which they are used in the book.

Aspect ratio – the relationship between length and breadth

Athwartships – across a ship

Barque – three or more masted sailing vessel square rigged on all masts except the after mast which is fore and aft rigged.

Barquentine – three or more masted sailing vessel square rigged only on the forward mast.

Brig – two masted sailing vessel square rigged on both masts

Bilges – technically that part of the inside of the hull between the topsides and the bottom planking, but also used for the lowest part of the interior where bilge water collects

Body Plan – the part of the lines plan which shows the shape of the ship as if the hull was cut through vertically like a loaf of bread

Boom – a long spar used to enable a sail to extend efficiently. Also a spar extended from a ship from which small boats are attached. Also a double ended Arab vessel, usually two-masted

Boot-top – that part of the underwater hull paint which shows above water

Bowsprit – a spar extending from the bows of the vessel to allow more sails to be set

Boxhaul – a process of tacking a sailing ship which includes a stern board

Brace – the controlling rope to the end of the yard

Brailing – the process of gathering a gaff or other sail into the spars on which it is set

Brigantine – a two-masted ship with a full stack of squaresails on the foremast and with a gaff or Bermudan rigged aftermast

Bunt – the full curved part of the middle of a sail

Buttock lines – short for bow and buttock lines – longitudinal and vertical hull sections

Carlins (or carlings) – pieces of timber set fore and aft in the deck as the edges of hatches and other openings

Caulking – the hammering of a filling material (usually oakum) between the plank edges of a wooden hull to make it watertight

Clamps – fore and aft members of a wooden hull used to help to secure the ends of the deck beams to the shipside

Clew – the corner of a sail, the bottom corners of a squaresail or the aftermost corners of a fore and aft sail

Clincher – the overlapping of planking when building a hull to allow the planks to be clenched together with fastenings

Close hauled – sailing as close to the wind as is practicable

Cross section – a section as if a hull has been cut in two to show the details of construction and accommodation

Curragh – a traditional Irish vessel, originally made of skins stretched and sewn over a wooden frame

Deadeye – a three holed sheeveless block, used with lanyards to tighten the main rigging. So called because of their likeness to skulls

Depth – the depth of the hull from the deck to the keel

Diagonals – a term used in the draughting of lines plans to define fore and aft sections which are not square to the centreline

Downwind – with the wind behind the ship

Draft – the depth of the lowest part of the hull from the waterline

Drogher – a slow, heavy craft

Floors – the cross structure above the keel

Forecastle – the foremost compartment of the ship below a solid deck. Often used as a term for the crew accommodation wherever it is situated

Gaff – a spar holding out the top of a fore and aft sail

Galley – an oared sailing vessel, or the ship's kitchen

Garboards – the planks closest to the keel of a ship

Greenheart – a heavy, dense and durable wood

Gunwale – the uppermost fore and aft stiffening members at the sides of open boats

Hanks – metal fitting used to attach fore and aft sails to stays

Hogging truss – ropes or wires attached to bow and stern which are tightened to stop a hull dropping at the ends

Hydrodynamics – the science of a vessel's relationship with water

Hydrofoil – a form immersed in water which moves up or down or from side to side due to the effects of the water flowing over it

Jib – fore and aft sail set ahead of the forward staysail

Jibboom – a spar which extends a bowsprit to allow further sails to be set

Keel – traditionally the centreline timber on which a wooden hull is built, but also now used for an underwater hull extension to improve the windward ability, and usually carrying ballast

Keelson – an inner timber fixed above the keel, to add strength and support the floors

Kiting – flying a sail like a kite instead of drawing it in taut

Knee – a naturally grown timber used to support two, often right angled, parts of a ship. May also be metal or laminated wood

Laminar flow – water flow close to the hull surface which moves in steady streamlines. In non-laminar flow the interaction of the hull causes local turbulence

Lateen – a triangular or quadrilateral sail hung from a long raking spar. An Arab sail also common in the Mediterranean

Leeboard – a board used on either or each side of a boat to counteract leeway

Leeward – the downwind side of a vessel (the side away from which the wind is blowing)

Leeway – the sideways drift of a ship to leeward caused by the wind. A component in the hull action when going to windward

Length:
   sparred length – the total length of the rigged vessel
   hull length (LOA) – the total length of the unrigged vessel
   registered length – the length between the main points of construction
   waterline length (LWL) – the length of the immersed hull
   keel length – the length of the keel as the main construction member

Liburnian – a Roman oared warship, descended from piratical galleys

Lines plan – naval architect's drawings to show the shape of the ship. The body plan shows the hull as if sliced vertically and the water lines show it sliced horizontally

Longitudinal – any major fore and aft component of the hull construction

Mizzen – usually the aftermost mast in a three-masted ship, the third mast in a four-masted ship, and the middle mast in a five-masted ship

Offsets – measured distances from the centreline and baselines to defined spots on the hull surface, used to convey form from the design office to the building yard

Parrel – a necklace of balls and spacers strung to enclose the open ends of gaff jaws or to hold a yard to the mast. In both cases the balls reduce the friction when the gaffs or yards are raised or lowered

Plotting – the action of marking off from dimensions

Polar diagram – shows the performance of a ship over a full range of wind directions and strengths

Poop – the highest enclosed part of the ship at the stern

Reaching – sailing with the wind coming more or less at right angles over the ship's side

Royals – squaresails set above the topgallants and usually the uppermost sails in a stack

Running – sailing with the wind directly behind the ship

Running rigging – ropes, wires and chains which are moved to control the sails

Scantlings – the sizes of the components of a ship

Schooner – two or more masted sailing vessel with each mast fore and aft rigged

Section – a vertical slice of a hull

Sheeve – a pulley wheel used in rigging

Shelves – the main fore and aft members of a wooden hull on which the deck beams lie

Ship (rig) – three or more masted sailing vessel with all masts square rigged

Shrouds – the permanent rigging from a masthead to the sides of a ship or from an upper mast to the mast beneath (having been spread by the top)

Skeg – a fixed extension of the hull immediately ahead of the rudder

Spanker – a fore and aft sail on the aftermost mast, and the mast itself in a five-masted ship

Stability – the ability of a vessel to resist heeling under different loads and sailing conditions

Staysail – fore and aft sail hanked to a stay

Sternpost – the post to which the rudder is attached

Stern board – the ship being sailed stern first as part of a manoeuvre

Strakes – lengths of skin surface, usually planks of wood

Stringers – fore and aft timbers of the hull construction normally fitted in way of the bilges although sometimes spaced around the hull envelope

Thwart – a plank used as a seat across a boat

Tonnage:
    displacement – the actual weight of the ship
    deadweight – the displacement when the ship is loaded to the maximum allowed
    gross – an assessment of the volume of the ship
    net and **registered** – an assessment of the volume of the ship available for cargo
    burthen – the weight of cargo which can be shipped
    Thames – an assessment of hull volume used for yacht racing
    tuns – the number of tuns of wine which can be carried

Top – the platform up a mast used to extend the side rigging and to give the crew access to the yards

Topsides – the sides of the vessel generally above water

Transom – the aft face of the hull

Truss – a metal fitting which holds the yard to the mast and allows it to rotate

Wale – a strake, usually of timber, along the length of the sides of a ship

Waterplane – the area of the hull which occupies the sea at the waterline

Windward – the side from which the wind blows

Yard or spar – a length of wood or metal to which a sail is attached

Zuga – a structural framework on the centreline under the thwarts of a Greek galley

FURTHER READING

The Jason Voyage
Tim Severin, Hutchinson, London 1985

The Ulysses Voyage
Tim Severin, Hutchinson, London 1987

The China Voyage
Tim Severin, Little, Brown, London 1994

The Brendan Voyage
Tim Severin, Hutchinson, London 1978

The Sutton Hoo Ship Burial
Rupert Bruce-Mitford, British Museum, London 1968

The Sindbad Voyage
Tim Severin, Hutchinson, London 1982

Matthew
Steve Martin & Colin Sanger, Godrevey, St. Ives, Cornwall 1996

The Voyage of the Matthew
Peter Firstbrook, BBC Books, London 1997

Bound Down for Newfoundland
Chris LeGrow, Breakwater, St. John's, Newfoundland 1998

Lord of the Isles Voyage
Wallace Clark, The Leinster Leader, Naas, Ireland 1993

The Mary Rose
Margaret Rule, Conway Maritime Press, London 1982

England Expects
Dudley Pope, Weidenfeld & Nicolson, London 1959

Life in Nelson's Navy
Dudley Pope, Chatham Publishing, London 1981

The Life and Times of Young Endeavour
David Iggulden, C. Pierson, Sydney, Australia 1995

The Charleyman
Eileen Reid Marcil, Quarry Press, Ontario, Canada 1995

INDEX

Aileach 11, 78-85
Aitken, Lady 125
Aitken, Sir Max 123
Alan-Williams, David 7
Anne, H.R.H. Princesss 110, 114
Argo 18-29

Beaverbrook Foundation 123
Beynon, Joe vi
birlinn 78,82
Blackwell, Mike 67, 68
Blake, Chris 141, 142, 147
Bloodhound 117
Bowles, Geoffrey 2
Brendan 42-50, 78
Bristol 63, 65, 67, 75
Britannia 152, 161
Brooke Marine/Yachts 141
Bruce-Mitford, Rupert 51

Cabot, John 63, 65, 66
Cadland Ship, The 161-163
Charles, H.R.H. Prince 140
Clark, Miles vi, 78
Clark, Wallace vi, 78, 79, 82
Cole, E & Sons 125
Contractor, Soli vi
Cutty Sark 103-105

Drummond, Maldwin vi, 139,
    144, 163
Dunbrody 92-102

Edinburgh, H.R.H. the Duke of
    68
Egan, John vi

Fincham 107

Gaches, Norman 2, 126
galleys 10, 11, 37, 39, 78-85
Gay, David 117
Gifford, Dr Edwin 51, 53
Goa Shipyard Ltd. 156
Greenhill, Richard vi
Groves and Guttridge 110

Hsu Fu 30-36

Indian Navy 119, 155, 156

Jarvis, Professor Mike 79
Jhellum 102
John F. Kennedy Trust 94
Jubilee Sailing Trust 121, 122,
    124, 125, 137

Kemmis Betty, Mark 126
Kent, Duchess of 141

Lance, Rod 153
Liburnian 37-41
lines plans 15-17
Lord Nelson 9, 15, 121-137, 141
    142, 143, 155, 156
Lord of the Isles 78
Lyddon, Lou vi

MacDonald, Andrew 78, 80, 83
MacDonald, Ranald 78
Macdonalds of Moville 83
Mainsbridge, Ian vi
Malcolm Miller 148
Marques 122
Mary Rose 70, 86-89
Maryport Trust 37, 39
Matthew 6, 14, 63-77
Millar, Max 103
Motivala, Homi 157
Munro, Charles vi, 123, 141, 147

Naish, George 2
Benn, Nathan vi
Newfoundland 44, 46, 63, 65,
    68, 71

Oliver, Thomas Hamilton 92

Pattursson, Trondur 80
Pope, Dudley 91

Queen, H.M. the 68, 152

Reidy, Sean 94
Royal Navy 9, 163
Royalist 2, 106-117, 119, 122,
    127, 128, 129, 136, 142

Rudd, Chris vi, 121, 122, 137

Sail Training Association 139
Saluz, Arthur vi, 23, 72, 93, 127,
    146, 151, 157, 163
Scott, Frank 157
Scott, Morin vi, 106, 107, 108,
    115, 121, 133
Sea Cadets 106, 107, 108, 110,
    119
Severin, Tim vi, 19, 20, 26, 27,
    31, 32, 34-36, 43, 44, 46, 48-
    50, 55-58, 60, 62, 78
Sindbad 55, 56, 58, 60
Sir Winston Churchill 148
Sohar 54-62
Soren Larsen 122, 124
Spencer, Harry 125
Stephens, Olin 140
Surfury 110
Sutton Hoo 51-53

Tarangini 154-160
Thatcher, Prime Minister 152
Three Quays Marine Services 156
Trajan's column 37, 39
Tunas Samudera 150-153

Uffa Fox 110

Varuna 118, 119, 142, 155
Victoria & Albert Museum vi, 37
Victory 86, 90, 91
Vosper Thornycroft 125

Waters, Sarah vi
Weller, Arthur 140
Wivenhoe Shipyard 125
Wolfson Unit, MTIA vi, 128, 140

Yachting World vi
Young Endeavour 138-149, 152,
    153, 155